LIKE BITS OF WIND

THE SWISS LIST

LIKE BITS OF WIND

Selected Poetry and Poetic Prose, 1974–2014

PIERRE CHAPPUIS

Translated by John Taylor

LONDON NEW YORK CALCUTTA

swiss arts council
prɔhelvetia

This publication has been supported by a grant from
Pro Helvetia, Swiss Arts Council.

Seagull Books, 2016

ISBN 978 0 8574 2 338 2

British Library Cataloguing-in-Publication Data
A catalogue record for this book is available from the British Library.

Typeset by Seagull Books, Calcutta, India
Printed and bound by Maple Press, York, Pennsylvania, USA

CONTENTS

INTRODUCTION

Translating Pierre Chappuis

Pierre Chappuis has remained unjustly absent in English, except for scattered translations in print magazines, online reviews and two anthologies, in contrast to other widely published key figures from a remarkable generation of French-language poets—Anne Perrier, Yves Bonnefoy, Philippe Jaccottet, Jacques Dupin, André du Bouchet, Jacques Réda and Pierre-Albert Jourdan—who have scrutinized what might be termed as 'the nature of Nature'. This book rights this situation by making available a representative selection of Chappuis's prolific *oeuvre*, ranging from his pioneering collections of short prose (*Blind Distance*, 1974) and short verse (*Full Margins*, 1997) to his most recent book of poetry, *Cuts* (2014). Long celebrated in his native Switzerland, Chappuis is one of the rare contemporary Swiss writers to be regularly published in France—with 15 titles produced by the Éditions José Corti, an iconic name in French publishing since 1925 because of its intimate association with Surrealists, as well as the writer Julien Gracq and other practitioners of 'high' literary styles. His writings delve into questions related to the essence of life, the notion of perception, the role of the perceiver and our relationship to landscape.

In regard to most of the aforementioned French-language poets, Chappuis examines Nature with the same intention—to capture its fleeting phenomena and deeper ontological structures. At the same time, he eschews metaphysical speculation, respecting his caveat in *The Proof Is in the Void* (1992), a volume of short texts about his own poetics, whereby 'metaphysical reflection [. . .], without contradicting poetry, will always remain outside it; outside that abandon, that sensibility, that part taken from words and from the singular experience provoking them, as well as that struggle.'

However closely one might wish to associate him with Jaccottet and du Bouchet—the former, because of analogous stylistic scruples; the latter, because of similarly acute perceptions—Chappuis's compositions reflect a sensibility and contagious passion all his own. He observes reality as sharply and is as sceptical of Romantic effusion as these peers, while something relatively uplifting exudes from his poetic prose (with its sinuous style and parenthetical inserts) and from his—in contrast—succinct, skeletal, haiku-like verse whose titles, like invigorating afterthoughts, are often placed at the end. While some French-language poets ponder on man's place in the cosmos and emphasize how human beings deceive themselves by desiring some kind of putative transcendent reality, Chappuis tends to accept this predicament or impossibility with less anxiety, at least as far as his texts are concerned: the narrator of his poems, whether merely implicit or, less often, asserted with a discreet 'I', is more likely to be a spectator recording heightened perceptions than one who is unable to describe outside reality without simultaneously reflecting on his troubled inner relationship with it. In 'Spiritual Progress', another short text about his poetics, Chappuis tellingly writes: 'Surpass—absolute incentive—what is personal in the emotion; the poem should surmount the emotion, lead it beyond itself until its own origin is forgotten.' The invigorating ambience of his writing partly stems from this 'absolute incentive'; one can sense his enthusiasm about going into the great outdoors in order to discover revelatory natural phenomena, and yet this exploratory elan is not overtly autobiographical. His enthusiasm becomes available to us all.

Chappuis's poetic explorations with regards to subjectivity and objectivity must be analysed while keeping an additional nuance in mind. In his collection of personal essays, *Muettes émergences*, literally 'Silent Emergences' (2011), he cautions himself, 'pas plus poème que chute d'eau'; to paraphrase, 'no more poem [must exist] than [there is] falling water'. It is the natural surge of falling water that matters. Poetry helps us to see more vividly and deeply, but its goal should be limited to revealing the natural phenomenon without embellishing it with words. This anti-rhetorical stance is typical of French-language poets with sensibilities similar to Chappuis's; moreover, the corollary project of discerning 'things-in-themselves' was formulated much earlier, notably by Francis Ponge, not to mention Rainer Maria Rilke and philosopher Edmund Husserl. Yet differences obtain between Ponge, the French 'thing-poet' par excellence, and his Swiss counterpart even when the latter similarly suspends subjectivity and lets his 'reverie be born of the very places' in which he strolls, as he proclaims elsewhere in *Muettes émergences*. In 'Everything except Dread', another essay in this same collection, Chappuis calls for the necessity of 'excavating, pushing on further—into [what is] darker, barer, more primary—ever further'. Although he can be terse in his verse (though rarely in his poetic prose), there is nothing grim or tight-lipped about the quest for the most elemental core that it is possible to perceive, or intimate, inside the natural 'thing' or phenomenon. Therefore distinguishing him from the poetics of 'thingness', of objectivity, of materiality, this desire to venture ever further into the 'darker, barer, more primary' ever accompanies the initial elan motivating him to go outside and, sometimes, to rise above, for he relishes hiking in the mountains.

This essentially applies to his texts about landscapes and natural phenomena. But the pursuit of 'darker, barer, more primary' reality 'behind' or 'before' appearances also sometimes occurs when the poet reflects on determining events from his childhood. One example is a poetic prose piece, 'The Birth of Uneasiness' (*The Black of Summer*, 2002), in which Chappuis recalls a sudden, significant, inner transformation that takes place while he is riding his bicycle:

What he thought he was heading for when he hit the road (*the summer, the beautiful carefree summer*), opposing forces slyly draw further away from him in order to stultify him all the more—harmful, gruelling forces even more invincible than the raging wind. Still ahead of him the same distance he has not yet covered.

Childhood irremediably wounded by this first crack through which infiltrates the plague of solitude.

The places, although the same, as they ever have been (*how have they been marred so quickly?*), and time, all bear the invisible mark of this. Will keep it . . .

Chappuis peers into the same kind of existential depths in other texts from both *The Black of Summer* and *Abstracted from Time* (first published in 1990, reprinted in 2005). At least one of these pieces is explicitly based on the composer Robert Schumann's life; the reader will, in fact, notice several allusions to classical music throughout this selection of Chappuis's work. 'Fatality of Water' stages the German Romantic composer's attempt to kill himself by drowning in the Rhine:

Unique, ultimate, an instant, a sound, dark gleam, whole, growing.

Ultimate, absolute, but an instant: he is embraced by the river, which he wants for himself ('*mine!*'), entirely ('*may your breathing be mine!*'), forever engulfed in its tumult.

The sounds ('*ah, the forces are everywhere unleashed against me!*'), all the sounds, are blended by the scarf of the river into a single scream carried beyond itself.

Words ('*Malediction, oh my burning reason!*') and thought killed before they are born, crushed (*dizziness and deafening roar*) by the vise gripping him . . .

Elsewhere in Chappuis's writings, dreams provide the impetus to the narrative. Once again, it is not the narrative details that are important—he does not relate the dream step by step—but, rather, his approach to the deep source of the dream. In other texts, he embarks on a journey with the intention of nearing the deeper sources of life. In *The Proof Is in the Void*, he notably writes apropos of the notion of 'resemblance': 'Echoes, reminders, recognition, what is similar restores life, prevents attaining anything unique.' This general principle is often illustrated in his writings. In *Blind Distance*, for example, 'All of a sudden, the echo yields to the morning, to the squawking of birds sheltering themselves beneath the arbour.' The word 'echo' in fact recurs frequently, like an echo of itself, and the poet is 'on the lookout' for them, as he states in 'Noon Fanfares' (*The Black of Summer*). Not unrelated to this characteristic aspect of seeking the source, Chappuis's poetics accentuates the use of blank spaces in poems and in the layout of some of his prose texts. He writes about interspersing blank spaces within the text in *The Proof Is in the Void*: 'Going down all the way to where there is nothing more to say, the origin and incentive that the poem is before words, that founds it, roots it (*taking away all roots*), throws it into language by means of an indraught.' Words make us return to the brink of the blankness, as it were, for this is where the 'origin' and the 'incentive'—the primeval elan that is life itself—can hopefully be found. Another way of contemplating this blankness is expressed in the following lines from 'Less Excess Brightness' (*Abstracted from Time*); speaking ceases and only light remains:

> Like bits of wind, the shadow gradually crumbles.
> With no speech, no voice; nothing but light.

Working closely with Chappuis on this book has been one of the delights of my career while the translation itself has proved to be one of the greatest challenges. Scores of email messages, letters, annotated manuscripts and postcards have travelled between us since 2012, and we have also met a few times in France and Switzerland —though much less for intense work sessions than for friendly conversations. Without the poet's amicable, untiring attentiveness to my questions, and without his wife Geneviève's participation—she has offered many invaluable insights—this translation would not have been possible.

Although some rare words appear in the original texts (my favourite being '*chape-chutent*' in a poem from *Cuts*, an obsolete term which I have rendered with the phrase 'swish down'), as well as some deliberate alliteration and consonance, not to mention a few instances where the same image intentionally depicts two parallel phenomena (for example, the 'flying seagulls' and 'moving waves' in a poem from *Full Margins*), the main challenge of rendering Chappuis's work involves the word order of his poetic prose. This syntactic issue is crucial as the poet often departs from colloquial naturalness and standard written usage in order to create certain effects. In tangible ways, the form—the syntax—is (also) the meaning of the text because the order of words attempts to mirror the rhythmic variability and the disjointedness or fragmentation at the very heart of our fugacious perceptive experience. In 'Discontinuity', another short text about his poetics, he offers an image of the kind of fundamental truth that his style not only must seek but also represent:

> Discontinuity, yet taken up in a movement; a rupture and the effacement of the rupture; fragmentation—each part has its own life, from which wells up the appetite for wholeness; discourse which follows no straight line, but which, in one way or another, whenever buried, rises to the surface.

Above all, Chappuis compares his prose to flowing water. In 'Eddies', he makes this analogy:

> The water near the shore gathers together and breaks apart into various smaller eddies, renewed, uncompleted. In order to express them, such is the sentence, the poem (awaited, forthcoming) with its suspense, its parentheses, its second thoughts. May beneath these opposing movements that harm each other, that destroy each other on the surface, reign a mass sweeping them along, bringing them into being, ensuring all continuity.

Likewise in 'Parentheses', which is a key text for understanding his stylistic aims, he states that his sentences flow 'like water, backing up here, rushing into a gully there'. In the same text he adds: 'Let's take leaps, fragmentation, and interruptions as essential elements for poetry, as well as the approach to the oneiric sources on which they might well depend, like a desire to follow in its apparent chaos the surging forth (I cannot say the flow) of thought (thought is not the right word).'

The reader of this anthology will necessarily meditate on words such as 'flow' and 'thought', let alone on other notions recalling the insights of the pre-Socratic philosophers who were likewise on the lookout for the 'first image . . . welling like a source', as Chappuis states in *Blind Distance*. In addition, seasonal change forms a rudimentary leitmotif that sometimes, as in *Full Margins* and *Cuts*, enables to poet to place his texts in a cyclical order. Besides the 'echo', a frequent image in this selection is that of the 'stream'. If readers initially infer that the flowing water, like Heraclitus' river, symbolizes an ontology of constant variability, they will be challenged, as they proceed, by the many allusions to 'sameness' in these texts. Chappuis's writing leads us to the fundamental notions of sameness, changeability, rest and movement; that is, precisely what we may dwell on while contemplating flowing water.

Chappuis's sentences are like watercourses that are subject to counter-currents and eddies and yet they remain fluid in the reader's mind. His poetic prose attempts to render this aqueous complexity, appealing not only to sometimes uncommon arrangements of words but also, characteristically, to parenthetical incises. Such inserts, at times italicized, enable him to reproduce the intricate, discontinuous, movements of thinking, of sensibility (for emotion is intimately engaged in the process)—and, ideally, the prose poem, taken as a whole, also forms a kind of music. One of the most significant, indeed extreme, examples is 'The Emptiness of Words' (*Blind Distance*), where the key word 'echo' appears only at the very end:

> Clayey, chalky, knotty, wave after wave all the way to the cliffs on the horizon; compressed, solidified, whirling, it extends like luminous mud, like silt, a blank page (*the emptiness of words*), sticking to the slopes, whitewashed again, cottony, licking the trees at my feet. Hardly separating me from it is the edge of the forest, entangled spruce trees from which seems to rise, like a tale—gaping, fringed, deep like night, like the rimaye cutting off a vast glacier flow, like the ground falling out from under the hiker's feet (*the emptiness of words*), unique, primeval, uncrossable—an echo.

The initial 'it' in the above text illustrates another feature of Chappuis's prose. He occasionally employs pronouns that simultaneously personify the natural phenomenon which they represent. For example, in 'The Diaphanous Shadow', a text included in *Within the Voice's Reach* (2002), he employs a feminine *elle* that evokes a 'river' (*rivière*, a feminine noun) as well as suggests a woman; whence the necessity of rendering *elle* with the word 'she', even though the English reader may thereby think that it alludes more to 'a woman' than to 'a stream' (whereas, arguably, the French reader will be able to keep both images simultaneously in mind):

> Her chest barely quivering, as if she were going to come to (*no, however*); her lips barely moving, sky or water, bearing the dawn.
>
> Diminished, the shadow is brightening, livening; noise of a scattered scintillation.
>
> Breathing softly, smiling, happy in her light sleep, wave after wave (*murmur fading away*), her dream is cradling her all the way to the heart of the reedy marsh along the lake.
>
> Amorous instability.

Some of these fragments possess sensual, even erotic connotations. However, this is not true with respect to the term *elle* in 'Memory Erased Proportionately' (*Within the Voice's Reach*), even though *mémoire* is also a feminine noun in French. Here the *elle* refers only to 'memory', not to a woman, and thus must be rendered by 'it':

> By heaps, rubbles, smudges, by sparkles, by masses, sun-like on the crack, relentlessly it pours out, dropping, sliding, slumping, bouncing back up, inexhaustibly feeding its fall. In vain, exulting, it furiously tries to shatter the daylight, to shatter itself, to ruin itself . . .

Chappuis and I have worked poem by poem through this subtle grammatical issue.

The not-readily-translatable aspects of his writing thus usually derive, not from words and expressions that have unsatisfactory equivalents in English but, rather, from the complex grammatical attributes of the French language. English is comparatively weak in its lack of most grammatical markers that French possesses, including feminine and masculine genders. To preserve meaning and coherency, the English speaker has to position semantically connected words quite closely together and often right next to each other. This has been the primary constraint during my work on this translation, and I have often tried to work my way around it. Although it was semantically impossible to re-create all of Chappuis's syntactic effects in English, I have taken some risks in the hope that the results will reflect his remarkably profound poetry and that the English-language reader will be 'greeted', as the author puts it in 'Ebb Tide', by some of the 'same enchantments'.

John Taylor
2 April 2016
Saint-Barthélemy d'Anjou

FULL MARGINS

I

All night long
the black leather notebook
has stayed open
to a blank page.

In the morning, snow.

(hiatus)

Such as,
in the very riverbed of winter,
pebbles stirred by an imaginary water.

Such as
when it seemingly stops,
imprisoned by the frost,
the exhausting din of the road.

(speechless space)

The plain beneath heaps of haze;
eyesight sliced by the north wind.

Surroundings on the run.

(jostling)

Between the trees
gleams
the gilded edge.

December dark and bare.

The evening has closed in on itself.

(at night)

On the move, very slowly.

Dead leaves and reflections.

Route itself wandering.

(*within distance itself*)

Faintly tinkling
the little bells of frost.

The gaze:
luminously, ever nearing,
swerving.

Slight,
slight beneath each footstep
are the cracks.

(morning)

Snowy rising of the light.

Each step casts off the previous one
that has entered the rocky roadbed.

In the daylight's liquid murmur
all noises dissolve.

(another morning)

A dive
from here
into the haze.

Woolly watery expanse;
lake rising
into daylight.

(hour and place uncertain)

A deserted street, another one:
cold is, in the hand,
the sky's ramp.

(presence of Pierre Reverdy)

Columns, wall, tomb

—and the same swallowing up of voices
as their echoes catch up with them.

The stream doesn't die
in its ice prison.

(*January*)

In the emptiness, this double note
—foggy outline—
sounds precise, sounds clear.

Remaining indefinable
—will they emerge?—
the edge and the top of the roof.

(titmouse before noon)

With no hold on the snow,
the shadow withdraws.

Naked is the flight of the crow.

Light, the day's water.

(*the February bird*)

Like a boat stem,
cleave the cold.

And not that, gleaming,
coming up to me first,
the cold could chop me.

Torrentially, the north wind.

(open sky, in February)

Digging,
delving into the twilight.

Upon us already, step by step,
the darkness.

(*narrow heart*)

And, swift-winged,
occasional space renovators
crossing invisible screens.

(in the blue)

So pale, afar,
almost faded.

(Daylight
in its transparency.

Daylight.)

Sky, lake.

(*even, equable*)

On the page of waters
in vain
you inscribe your flight

Dual bird
chasing yourself

(fleetingly)

II

Porous, vaporous,
the mountains stand back.

Blurring,
the horizon dulls
into transparency.

Mountains of dream, of haze:
words unburdened of their meaning.

(*bevelled mirror*)

First, on high
opens out
a fan of flames.

Soon everywhere the same blazing.

(open sky)

First rain, barely
—barely a little coolness.

First trills,
uncertain, intermittent,
between the loosened stitches of the night.

Will become song
at the edge of emptiness.

(another day, same hour)

Grey, still grey,
the tumult of the storm
wanes.

The rain!

May roof and pillars
collapse.

(*March wreckage*)

Shadow
(water)
shattered by daylight.

Or
(be they reeds)
screeching.

(sparkles)

Greyness,
grey flying, cheeping.

Screeching.

Sweeping about with a broom
in all directions
to scatter the March ash.

(cloud effect)

Clear surging among the pines

—too lively, wholehearted
to be a cheerful stream
happy to be crumpled
uncrumpled at leisure.

Rustling through the daylight.

(estuary of the wind)

Quicklime,
at night
beneath the thick foliage
reviving.

Whiteness shining forth.

(evening)

Like many green clumps;
like a bouquet of umbels.
Like snow.

And, in the coolness,
breath or dream,
this lightening.

Clouds
having come to crown our night.

(at your side)

Their hemmed
initial whiteness.

Unattached, they move forward,
chimerical double of the mountains.

Summer bearers
jubilant.

(first lovely days)

Here, there,
unexpectedly,
their crests stick up
and fall back down.

Chasing each other
lovingly,
lying down again
in the wind.

(seagulls or waves)

In shreds,
the thin wall of brushwood!

Lake and sky in unison,
liquid.

Through the slightest crack
daylight besieges me,
budding.

(*indraught*)

Blackish, scattered.

Their cawing doesn't scratch
the April snow.

(crows in the morning)

Snow at dawn on high,
April tidewater.

Acute, airy,
with a single stroke,
like bird cries,
outlining peaks and combes.

(open sky, once again)

Smooth ground
the first pollens
enliven
like scattered joy.

As best they can,
your footsteps adjust
to the day's flagstones.

(*into the blue*)

Dust, no,
nor is it hail
or snow.

Feathers falling
as if from a torn-open eiderdown.

(cherry tree in April)

Streaking ahead,
cutting through the waves
all the way to the last whiffs of light
in high altitude.

Here
—like a beating pulse—
the blue of the irises.

(even scales)

III

With smooth stretches, with dimples,
with puckers.

Sliding along,
smitten by its own force.

A stream, blazing furnace.

At eye level,
the sun has gone back to bed.

(*vanishing point*)

Rain—to speak
through the foliage
without raising one's voice.

Leaves—to smooth out
word by word
the worn silk of their brooding.

(*May, the month of May*)

Close
surveillance of the water
and the sky nearby.

Flying in veers, in swerves.

Crossing, criss-crossing
the stitches of the wind
as far as the eye can see.

(*swallows, recovering their territory*)

With a stroke, with a shriek, every which way
taking out the tacking threads from the wind.

Playful
arrogant swallows
panicked by an invisible obstacle.

(idem)

Smooth in its speechlessness,
the vast plain of the daylight
opens out.

Slack, motionless,
yet with no fixed point,
like one coming back to oneself.

                                                    (*anew*)

Fording.

Haze and light,

from these heights draped
to the other shore—invisible.

The gaze hardly alights.

(*in one stroke*)

Beyond the haze,
gently,
the mountain climbs back up its slope.

Vaguely,
in the heat,
sways.

(from the window)

Stars in summer
in the trees.

Trills,
night-time outbursts.

(*before the whole night*)

Calls and responses
cry out above our heads.

Laths—your support, where is it?

Musical roof frame
ever being renovated.

(*mentally, Paul Klee*)

Wall
like, at eye level,
the base of the night
blocking the view.

(non-place)

Steeple, willows,
jagged shore.

Children's luminous
outbursts.

Impalpable hubbub.

(*a whole*)

At high noon,
in summer,
they are walking through the snow.

At the edge of the road
sparkles
a gravel pile

—a pothole.

(July, high up)

Cut wheat.

The light, on the ground,
carries the night.

(midsummer)

Ice
at the heart of summer.

The darkness
of devouring daylight.

Heat
like a raised stone.

(split in two)

Shadow, daytime ink
like a brushwood made
of golden-headed needles.

Will you last, rampart,
with your thousand open cracks?

Anthracite is such dense
daylight, ready to explode.

(*daylight fluting through*)

Gleeful

gulls have alighted,
as if at the edge of the path,
on a line of reeds
they crease for the pleasure of it.

(propitious white stones)

Taut all day long
the bow of the summer
—noises and echoing sounds—
joins the two extremes.

Motionlessness of the heat.

(sonorous space)

IV

The clearing, its harrow of shadows,
now are swept away
with the stroke of a broom.

Fluffy volutes;
soon
moving wall.

Above, the azure.

(*new page*)

Scratching for the pleasure of it,
incorrigibly,
the windowpane of the fog.

(*starlings above the vineyard*)

Walking
against the wind, the white sky,
against the sun.

In an instant,
instead of the hillside to climb,
opens up a neckline.

Under the trees
the daylight falls in golden raindrops,
like seed.

(flamboyant)

Blending
luminously
gold and azure.

(*larches*)

Where from?

In the aspens, sizzling.

Brief fire,
glimmer blown out by the wind.

(*half-seen*)

Quick, quick!

—The ground
ah! The elasticity of the ground!—

Already the greyhounds of dawn
at the back of the combe
are bounding.

(the heart at ease)

Autumn ablaze,
the wind under the open sky,
in fits and starts.

Debris
(like tiles)
strewn over the path
and the stream.

(*November wreckage*)

Clouds reared up at roof level.

That gallivant,
stragglers in a frantic retreat
despite the diminished space.

In the wind's neckline
beats—not at all for them—
the metronome of rain.

(new cloud effect)

Dark, without a hitch,
driving along at the appointed time
through the gloomy swamps.

The noise grows fainter.

Unscathed is the evening's lining.

(while thinking of a friend)

Whining, cantankerous,
still on the job
despite nightfall.

Row after row,
with a nicked ploughshare,
they scratch the shadow.

(crows at twilight)

Crows in flight
like paper being crumpled.

(more or less like yesterday)

Splendour!—

And the last tatters of night
remain snared
in the sweater of the snow.

Woolly is the cawing.

(*November, in the vineyard*)

Pond,
dull greyish-green mirror.

Every image blurry.

(twilight)

Sheet-metal bird
high in the sky.

Piercing, luminous,
its cry grows faint
and is smothered
by the icy twilight.

(December once again)

At the height of expectation,
turning with the slightest wind,
rusty, husky-voiced, grating.

Ah!
The shadow's multiple directions!

The lost refrain of the night,
no,
it won't be pieced back together.

                                        (*in uncertainty*)

Being alleviated,
shadow zone after shadow zone.

Its torpor, or ours.

From west to east
the sky, all day long,
stays ahead of us.

(gap)

Mute, not moved

—there, in front of me,
absorbs the daylight.

Water.
Well.

Lake or abyss.

A trace,
like the line of dawn,
broken off, does not vanish.

(the same for words)

BLIND DISTANCE

. . . Sameness gathers difference into a primeval union. What is equal, on the contrary, scatters some simply uniform oneness into the bland unity . . .

. . . Memory, fluid simulacrum . . .

. . . Image echo reflection of a perpetual birth . . .

The Opposite of Insomnia

In the depths (*so motionless one's ears prick*), in the very depths of night a clearing opens. (*My sleep, this tower.*) I awake as if at the heart of a pinewood. Uncertain and peaceful (*perhaps a noise*), unheard of, shrill (*or when I approach?*), whimsical, monotonous (*thin blades*), light-hearted and free, and nonetheless ever led back to the same twirling (*this thread on which I depend*), to the same halts above emptiness (*constantly snaps again wherever tied back together*), the sound of a flute rises all the way up to my silent room. (*My dream, this fragrance.*)

Moving Motionless

Puffed out by the wind, the chestnut trees of the terrace are glimmering in the night. From the fog spread out into light wisps (*foam, but from swelling waves that have calmed down, seed, residue*) emerge shadowy balls drifting towards the moving fringes of the expanse (*a barely distinguishable negative, coastal navigation in shallow waters*).

Ancient Hierarchy

Until now fidgety and noisy, the lark stops moving. Its song breaks off like wind dropping and the countryside stands transfixed (*a thousand passionate pleas, with shouts and fragrances echoing in the silent nave*), organizing itself around an unreal, imperceptible point while awaiting the just and vertical fall.

The First Image

Fleeing in all directions, fur gleaming in the sunlight, the sprawled-out dog, silent fox hunt! (*No, no: simply chasing, as in a game, the same sequence ever repeated.*) Yet, first, the field of light! The flies buzzing around me, drill chasms into it which close up just as soon. Awakening (*the stinging wind, tiny embers on the skin*); momentum (*both absorbed in the motley coloured meadows on the hill across from me and ceaselessly scouring the countryside*); waiting (*motionless like a fixed point in the joyous scuffle*). The scattered shadow of one cloud, then another (*groping like a wandering hand*), is slowly gliding along, and the first image comes back whole; will soon come back, again welling like a source.

Like the Summer

What place, what room without walls is never crossed nor occupied by anything, not even coolness? I am only drifting, immersed in luminous water, the same limit never gone beyond. Bound I am by voices coming from below, now silent—friendly or not, joyous, fraternal, transparent like the summer about to surge in the depths, in the uttermost depths of night, and like impossible bursts of laughter.

Like a Cry

Like a cry (*from where? from whom?*), the whirlwind
of lightning flashes. The night shaken, shoved down,
shaped back together in order to be grasped again
(*passing guest, stranger groping amid the furniture*),
savagely seized time and again. Outside, fields and vil-
lages flare up. Sallies, leaps, dehiscent night (*what other
sound further on?*), glimmers over the shredded land
(*groaning or howling?*), fractions engulfed before being
joined end to end (*or scrap metal crashing?*), getting to
the other side of the abyss. The relentless gale blasts
down on the poplars, the trodden gardens. Like the fab-
ulous bird (*sleeper once again swathed in the dream*), the
rain, in the greyish beginnings of the morning, will come
only when calm is restored.

The Enclave of Shadow

An enclave within the transparency of the plain, the shadow is shivering. An almost submerged island (*one path, the same one*) whose drifting I delight in following; an oblique forest gliding behind me towards emptiness. I plunge into the tatters of vegetation (*on the ground, a fire's reddish glow*), into the kingly vegetation, further on (*once caught up with, vanishes*), still further on (*on the ground, rot*), in the thickness, the noise of leaves stirring, of deadwood snapping, dazzled as if I were walking in the light (*the stuffy night heavier, however*).

Up to There

Up to that place (*the wind, the coolness*), meadow (*the high grass*), clearing of daylight (*the love-struck lark in the cloud*) crossed and not crossed by the path. Up to there (*the lark now out of sight*).

Late Fall

Emerges just in time, hollowed out, striped with shadow and glimmering (*the rows of espaliered trees, the panes of window frames*), as if raised above the mist-covered greenhouse (*aerostat, hot-air balloon of November*), the hillside clouded over at the top by an orchard of trees that are already black, in front of the other leafless ones, except for an apple tree still covered with its fruit. Chinese lanterns of a party now over, paled gleams that the sun revives by melting the frost deposited at night on their redness.

At the Limit

At the limit, or almost; in the fog cut by the snow-shovelled road, pierced by orchards. Beyond, the still-white rooftops move, come closer. Beyond, nothing. I am surrounded by the day. The mountain slope has toppled over: no end, no summit for the birdsongs unfurled from this height already almost in the sunlight?

The Balance of the Daylight

Brought back to this level path, I am walking by an orchard at the limit of the fog. Laundry hanging between trees; a crumbled wall that no longer encloses. Below, as if hatching, the noise of cars driving through the cluse. Higher up, a dazzling birdsong. I think I am touching, I am indeed touching the screen of the light, the espalier, the facade whose top is perhaps already gleaming. No more village, despite the background noise, despite gonglike hammering on a piece of sheet metal. Pathless, I proceed; on this path running past the houses, the only street, among the frosty pastures, running past the grey wall of the morning, among the ploughed fields—night pulled back against the ground and turned over. In the thundering sunlight, the bird alights on the roof.

November

Glorious, solar, ethereal (*and the room in which I write is neither confined nor vast*), the maple tree in front of the window is wearing itself out. The morning satisfies the appetite, shines forth (*the ink given back to the daylight*), submerging the room (*this yellow*), unlimiting it (*my very page*).

Non-hike

Having left behind the stream flowing beneath the day-light at the bottom of the gorge, I am climbing back up the ravine whose gleams are smouldering right on the dead leaves, right on the flaming snow. At the top, the slack hour is met with again. Grass and pebbles emerge, undoing all whiteness except off in the margin where I stand. Not a single footstep, not a single rut. A non-hike—what a delight!—following no path, towards the forest invaded everywhere by light. The shadow below, the plain with its snow melted away reappear. A neutral hike, along level ground, guided by what lack, what source?

Mountain Flying

Zeppelin already in the sunlight, emerging once the embankment has been climbed, then moving off proportionately, white, new, forgotten until it fades away behind the hazy forest. The snow here sticks to the branches like glue.

Esplanade

The dawn's pavement, an esplanade, yet vast, a new field, all parallel cracks solidified. Far ahead of me, a motionless, yellow, Saharan sun is growing hazy, but because of excessive cold. Chilling wind cuts into my face. Disorderly ridges, striae have vanished early, less fluffiness (*the earth as if swept out from beneath my feet, with no tracks left*); flames of snow brief and briefer (*absent flames*) streak away along the ground, far, fast.

Initial

The skyline as if slightly inflected, the water's slow breathing hardly bothered by the thousand darts of rain, the coots swimming at random add to this, equal themselves out. Should the still barely coloured branches of a willow (*initial, the mist wiped away*) surge, one's eyes, struck, will need to be sharpened again.

A Feast, No

A feast, no. But, at this moment (*peak, vastness*), the flame of the first star, the clear gaze into the evening. (*The whole sky, that wisp of straw.*) At this moment when the palms of night are weakly waving, when the fragrant shadow is thickening in the acacias, it's higher up, rather than here, that I would like to walk.

Hazy, Watery

In the greyish haze where the earth is coming undone, splitting up, ending, well past the iron bridge that shakes whenever trains cross it, I am heading down to the mouth of the stream. Cranes are dully scraping the fog (*the hammering of pieces of sheet metal, rust in the eyes*). Aimless walk amid the alluvium, the scrap metal, the bulldozers. A few yards away, a moorhen, the last one, swims to the right, to the left, dips its head into the water, plunges into indistinctness.

Like First Foliage

Rain, wind, March surging as I cross a torrent not impris-
oned by any streambed and then plunge into the beech
woods. Despite the clustered trees, the hillside appears—
skinny, pale, scabby. Drowned out by gusts of wind,
feeble birdsongs emerge as if they were first leaves.
The ground is strewn with blown-down branches like
shadows rising in tiers all the way up to the ridge of light.
I climb up towards the plateau where strong winds,
sunlight, and raindrops instantaneously becoming snow-
flakes, all are swirling.

Garden of Delights

From the same belvedere once again, watching out for the joining of day and night; watching out for the mingling of the waters, savouring, not savouring the cool wind. No spasm, which would undo the waiting. All around, the oaks are rustling. Already the depths of the plain are darkening. Already, with one signpost after another falling, the trees are hovering like shadows. Already daytime murmurs are blending into a slow, monotonous stridulation. Already the whole, shadowy, uniform land is changing into a blind and luminous garden of delights where one can walk right in.

Rigging

At the back of the room (*that hole the domesticated shadow cannot conceal*), cloistered in the half-light (*the widest opening*), I savour time without time passing by. High in the sky (*a steady noise, long-lasting*), the swallows are swirling. All the way to the horizon (*open the solid wooden shutter*), amid the chattering (*the wheel of the sun*), the wheat is shimmering. Perhaps I am moving forward, being swept along (*a quivering runs over the lips of noon*), perhaps, blinded (*the same noise again, weaker*), I have sunk into an abyss of light. Not the slightest shade except that borne by the rigging of the scattered trees on the hillside.

Blind Distance

High cloud cover, ablaze. All of a sudden (*what shutter pushed?*), I walk onto the threshing floor of the summer. Would the earth itself be this chaff blowing every which way? Around the village (*the hustle and bustle, the noise of the tractors, the threshing machines*), the same revolution is being accomplished. Deployments (*fervour, plain blurred with daylight*), order slowly being created or coming undone (*the swathes, the rows of raked-up hay*), luminous gravitation (*yet huddled together closely, the fields jostle each other*), ardour regulated by rows of poplars at the edge of the paths. (*Equable, my passion,—and the distance.*)

Chessboard of Vegetation

Walk unwearied into the coolness of the plain, with its wet soil smell. The shadow is thickening not at all. Every-where, among the clustered trees, the same pleas chirped by birds and the same answers, the same sodden paths and the same crossroads, the same paths cut straight through the forest and the same cloud cover. On the trails boring through the thickets, leaves stick to the face: the densely woven branches, and the high grass crushed noiselessly underfoot, slow down the hike. An unequal combat. There is nothing more delightful, however, despite my fleeting wish to beat a retreat. The narrow trail vanishes. With my hands and arms, I clear a path that closes up behind me. Water is pouring down in buckets from the leafy boughs. Walk unwearied towards the clearing where a woodcutter's fire is charring.

From the Top of the Twilight

Once again, beneath the oaks, as if, from the top of the twilight (*haul myself all the way up there*), I was following the return and the fulfilment of the same hour. Calmness extended to the four corners of the horizon, with the mountains moving away (*no longer straw flaming on the field at high noon*!). The clouds are fraying in the powdery evening crossed by the last swallow's jagged flight, while the land lays out the same hilly countryside as yesterday, as the day before yesterday. On the move (*in vain—but the destitution*! *but the disenchantment*!—*in vain I take inventory of them*), on the move, and the fire in the stacked-up shadows! Under a sky now again serene, the wandering resumes. (*Your words, hoist them into the night*!)

Before Daylight

A shadowy mountain ahead of me. The forest bursts into pieces (*or perhaps an absence that is too deep*). Drowning out, who knows what, nearby noise, moaning or baying, the wind is fraying the poplars at the edge of the path, sweeping over land on which false moonlight is shining between two gunshots, rushing into the bedroom. (*Onerous waiting, not really: ricocheting in the night.*) What's the use of staying on the watch, of wishing, through the tulle of the storm, to put back together what is coming undone from one lightning bolt to another? Having blindly groped my way back to bed, remaining attentive to the first signs of a lull (*the path cut through the forest opens and keeps opening again*), I wear out my wakefulness. In the hollow of the wind, rain softly begins to fall.

The Emptiness of Words

Clayey, chalky, knotty, wave after wave all the way to the cliffs on the horizon; compressed, solidified, whirling, it extends like luminous mud, like silt, a blank page (*the emptiness of words*), sticking to the slopes, whitewashed again, cottony, licking the trees at my feet. Hardly separating me from it is the edge of the forest, entangled spruce trees from which seems to rise, like a tale—gaping, fringed, deep like night, like the rimaye cutting off a vast glacier flow, like the ground falling out from under the hiker's feet (*the emptiness of words*), unique, primeval, uncrossable—an echo.

Above the Shadow

Above the shadow, higher, in the open air, building up, breaking up (*and words seem useless*). Splashing, ruins. The lustral seawater flowing overhead or the chalky mountain shining through the velvet of the evening, a lofty fronton of foam (*and eyes wash themselves with such water*).

Card Castle in the Morning

Commotion in the narrow, stingy November night. As if at the top of the hill the site of the future, the unique dwelling place of day, were being staked out. Chirped pleas from a blackbird. Tent raised in a blink. Dark lantern. Sides. Once again like a pyramid whose apex alone would emit light. What panic-stricken weather-vane? Fallen from a lantern of the dead, a semblance of light. Slight noises, stealthy steps, everywhere, on the scaffoldings. And nothing. A thousand preposterous projects. In any case, for the time being, reconnaissance is going on. But if only whims were yielded? Blind stubbornness? Portico. Shelter. Palace exposed. Collapsed walls. The vague desire to get up, to let myself be guided towards the morning, is leaving me. Smothered pleas are being taken back by the night on the threshold of sleep.

Daytime, Daily Life

Bigger after crossing the forest, the sun still at my height in the trees. Fog, narrower field: lacunae in the manuscript (*the frost of the dream*) straining the eyes deciphering them again. The straw of the first heat flares on the heights. Held above the silence (*all the land and more than the land*), a sporadic song is shining.

Clearing

Like water between ill-joined staves (*but it's daylight*), it seeps—broken off, split up, scarred—between the tree trunks, bursts, joyously lacerating the shadow, gashes, nicks, beams, here and there brightens up some birdsong at the heart and the edge of the clustered trees, expands like a window towards which, from the back of the room, I could walk, now spreads out like the luminous spine of the sky, like an unhemmed sheet, like a bare roof. By no means breaking off the pace, it makes one single sparkle, a future clearing (*my sentence*), sparkling, all minced up (*my impossible sentence*), at the heart, on the edge, not dividing, delighted, not deciding between whatsoever, but, as I approach, it becomes snow, a brimming over, an awakening.

Facing the Storm

Facing the storm, at the edge of emptiness, the fiery team of horses surges forward from the fountain basin. All of a sudden, the air has cooled. The neighing of the wind in the oaks drowns out the noise of the waterfall. From the horizon, clouds are flowing upward. Glimmers, bounds, are fleeing every which way just ahead of the gust beating down furiously at the wheat, the forests, the poplars with their dishevelled manes. The eyes blur. Big drops of rain are falling on the terrace where the whirlwinds have ceased. The fountain team rears up in vain, the lightning bolt rips the canvas cloth of the twilight in vain. Behind the theatre of the storm, daylight is tipping over into the darkness.

Empty-Eyed

Against the sunlight, down below, the plain vanishes, an expanse crossed by isthmuses. Water there? No. No shimmering water. The sunlight dwells in the highlands. A lifeless zone ahead of me, my searching eyes gaze emptily from the nearby hill to the nearby oak woods, to the cliffs closing off the horizon. Return, take up the same position, return again. And again.

From one edge to another. In the open air (*the same pillars*), in the light flowing among the trees. Paths and crossroads burrow themselves away (*the same nave, if the screens of vegetation were taken away*); the hour is turning round and round. Everywhere under the grey sky run the same paths cutting straight through the forest (*the next footsteps lighter*), everywhere, outdoors (*the fields, the vineyard-covered slopes bristling, and the water*), everywhere curtains, rows of trees linking farms and localities, draw back, come back together.

All of a sudden I enter the realm of winter (*the sinking sun*), a serene, smooth valley sealed by highlands (*snow, plateau as a turning hub*). Bouncily stepping along, I am hiking on staked-out, picketed paths, the mirrors of January at hand. Boundary marking, expanse. Clear, new, large (*blinding whiteness reigning alone*), the cold is invading me. Just blossoming through the snow, nervures of a different land emerge (*the mountains, the aerial plateaus soon beyond reach*), seeds and stubble lying in more or less straight lines, more or less thwarted by old wagon ruts, and run onward into the wind.

Time Erased

Facing the east (*the shadow having been swallowed*), just where the forest ends (*the shadow having been leapt across*), rises the mountain of ash. Exact, unexpected (*on the edges, the villages nestled in whiteness*), the host, the enemy comes down from the heights on which he was camping, occupies the levelled plain. But he who has relinquished these places is silently governing them. Subjacent land (*all the old patchworking*) that is evanescent, re-emergent, motionless and has seemingly flown off. Rolling around itself inside its glass bell, the rustling of the captive night reverberates in the morning.

Another Morning

Hollows of shadow and cold. The crunching snow. Joyous voices bursting out, probably near the swamp where people are skating. The almost frozen stream apparently leads there across the fields (*scissure*, *striature*). From the valley, numbed with cold, to the mountains, to the hills already bathed in sunlight, nothing known or unknown, similar or dissimilar. Exact, but *not quite exact*: pink variant of the preceding morning.

Spark

A curry comb? An overturned harrow? Nothing brings me closer (*eclipse or failure?*), nor could do so (*impalpable screen*) even if I were in the same place as that morning (*the dishevelled sheets upon waking*), touching, or almost, the same vineyard plots, again finding one after another the villages tiered up the slope, the snow (*ah! a footstep into emptiness!*), the snow as if boxed up, as if placed in bottle racks (*no*), in a recently spatterdashed cellar (*no, not really*).

Coppices, Clustered Trees

Opaque sky against the sunlight, water freezing in the swampy areas at the sides of paths without ruts. This cold is stirring up a fire in me. Through the undergrowth, I approach the pond. Every now and then the frosted bridge reappears through the gaps. Beneath the bell of daylight, highlands or clouds are shimmering at the outermost reaches. A few isolated birds' chirpings break out, seemingly rebounding. Coppices, clustered trees, though barren, surround me. The noise of the gravel pit has faded away. In the reeds, at the edge of the pond that remains remote, perhaps burst out the laughter and the shouting of children. I am walking in the noon light, from one lapse of silence to the next.

The Harrow of Eyesight

Water suddenly overflowing the banks on my left (*caresses, brief outbursts, silent lips*). I would have turned my back (*the barren trees*), I now would walk in the opposite direction (*the sodden path*) on a parcel of land seemingly washed away by the current (*the stream, and the stream*). At the end, as if leaving a hallway, I take up my position again (*the pebbly shoal, the high, the low*), invaded by daylight brushed back by the harrow of eyesight.

Blind in the Whiteness

Again against the wind (*the streaks in the soil, the tracks left by gusts*), with the forest set back to my right, I am climbing. Rebounds occur, in all directions. Blind in the whiteness, I am hiking across a plain. The snow-covered hedges no longer divide it, nor the snowdrift barriers placed along the roads, removable openwork fences for the emptiness. (*Within the whiteness, unbound.*)

False Witness

I am heading against the west wind. The road down below plunges into the fog. Slowly coming towards me is the hillside, and the sloping forest to my right. Brush-wood dragged towards the daylight, lazy cawing crows already on their search. The path vanishes halfway up the hillside. Illusions, the clods of earth, the stiff grass I am crushing underfoot. Or the frost. Fire gushes forth from the haze in the east. Short race to be the first to reach the hairy loin of dawn. The sky, the treetops, even the talus are all turning pink. The whiteness is gradually fading away.

Like Silent Water

Dark, calm, colourless forests in the wind. The pasture
as one single glistening (*fog, my naked dream*); stardust
shining beneath the moist grass (*my night buried, resorbed,
my vigil*). The sky is growing pale (*the soil moulting, like
summer frost*) and the drinking trough, the heap of stones,
once again emerge. On the nearby hills (*at the edges, the
first reddening*), the forests are taking up their positions
again.

Blank Page

In the milky night, my bearings lost, I am neither walking (*shadowy path denying my footsteps*) nor standing in the wind (*higher up, the rustling fringe of the cornfield*), nor getting up. Levelled out and depthless, the land in the moonlight can be read like a watermark. The whiteness and silence are unburdening me. The hillside is swelling like a luminous sail. (*My bearings lost, and still wandering within the absence*). Covered with stubble, the ground has vanished, luminously. In the distance, the gentle mountain, an anonymous nascent desire, almost appears.

Imperious Rutting

Once beyond the flaming curtain, the cold takes hold. Sky and water are both shining in the sunlight. Insane, this bird that has ventured over to this side, fighting against a torrential current! I can hear and cannot hear the breaking sound, the crackling aspen leaves. Standing, stirred up, the water is marching to the shore. I am moving forward with the wind over the pebbles. Free violence, imperious rutting, devastation, insatiable! To the devil the shelter of the plain, behind the fringe soon burned red by November! Haughty or fascinated, the brazen seagull is struggling at my level. Flipping over, it vanishes for a moment before swooping down with open wings onto the crest of a wave, seemingly struck by lightning, after thousands of others, and now gleaming.

The Noon Room

Sudden opening, after the narrow edge of autumn: light everywhere (*motionless water*) in the mirrors of the haze. Stirring up the chalk-white pebbles (*the noise of my footsteps, from one partition to another*), I walk alongside the shore all the way to its farthest point. In the distance, confusedly (*the liquid retaining wall of fog*), by the sea or up on the heights, a new city is gleaming, or a harbour (*a lake rising vertically*), or a gathering of seagulls. From a sparkling point (*stone, stiletto scratching the windowpane*), here and there, ever elsewhere the horizon is drawn, broken when the luminous bird, by veering (*sudden fit of energy, gasping*), discovers the shadow he bears under his wing. (*On my eyelid, fire.*)

Scattering

Higher up, down below, the light is moving through the openwork fence of night. Ah! its repercussion by successive patches (*chalk steles*) on the other side where the arch of looking wavers, gets another hold! I am walking among the pebbles (*here, where I have weight*), and the water is gradually being extinguished, burying dark sparkles.

Presently

Detours, slopes climbed up or down, the distance always re-establishing itself ahead of me, the shadow ever re-thickening. At last the stones of the path are sparkling like water and, at the limits (*to find myself there once again*), the horizon is knotting itself back together. (*To be there, presently.*) Down in the valley, an auburn sun is trembling: an extinguished fire, a tawny peat bog (*imperceptible, from here, are the shovelled-out ditches, and, in the reaches, the black water of childhood*), a pothole, moving depths that are consumed, within the November overgrowth, by the white aerial flame of the birches.

Placeless, Dateless

Unless I keep walking along the edge, a hiker whose own footsteps lead him onward (*in his midst, silence*), who is enchanted (*in his midst, the shadow soon undone*), the noise of the pebbles here and there jostled inadvertently, playfully.

Ebb Tide

From the same high spot (*this landscape, yesterday*), I greet the same enchantments (*yesterday towards evening, solemnly*), the same promises. Noon lightness. From the wild cherry trees to the wheat fields (*the hedge, the same hedge*), everything is now a luminous echo, cheeping, everything is clarity, impulse (*the wing of silence, flapping*), everything is distinct: orchards, meadows, stretches of vegetation (*yesterday, what glorious sequence of events, towards night-time?*) and, on the edges (*yesterday, what anchored ships?*), villages and forests that are being unfurled within the daylight. (*What forests, vaster yesterday? What masses now vanished?*)

What Bedroom?

What forest or what bedroom, what plain swept across by the storm? Sudden breaking and entering, nearby, kindled by the July heat: sweating, suffocation. I am groping my way towards the window. The lightning strikes the slope of the mountain rising in front of me and strikes again further on. An echo reverberating from the top to the bottom of the valley, or whirling on the plateau? Perhaps also fading out on the heights. All of a sudden, the echo yields to the morning, to the squawking of birds sheltering themselves beneath the arbour.

The Wheel of the Harvests

I would have turned like the shadow of the pear tree, alone in the middle of the hillside. The bushes of the nearby hedges, like the lark's hoarse song, are shimmering. In every moment, silence is closing around the buzzing of the flies or the horseflies, and the motionless heat is hugging me. At the farthest reaches, the mountains stand back in their transparency.

Image or Place

Down there in front of me (*the windowpane of the wind*), trembling and moving about. Flaring out. In front of me, motionlessness. Speckled image (*poplars in a row; elsewhere, trees bordering a field*); so familiar (*all paths trodden*), so different (*plain crossed so often*); which, if exalted, would float over the surface of the waters, smoothly, lightweight, as it left the shore. Once again, the place is beyond reach. At the extreme reaches of desire. May it be a cloister for me, equal to warmth. Joy between its walls of light or silence, wavy (*the windowpane of June*) as if the hay drying on the ground were, invisibly, in flames, porous crumbly walls through which the warbler bores openings. A step taken (*the gap*), then another. A trill, then another.

Another Lark

A muddle (*the warp and woof of looking*), a medley of colours, a thousand knots and strands of all lengths. My own tracks fade away proportionately. The silence grasped in one go refreshes me, the whole plain (*the changing sky, the field of May, the noon heat*) is at hand. A cry is shimmering in the cloud, a call, or a hundred calls: a lark astray, wordy (*fidgety flight and cry*), vanished, come back, multiple in its panic, ever elsewhere, rerouted (*blind? dazzled?*), suddenly silent.

August Orchard

No longer can I use the few lights shining on the plain as landmarks and the network of byways, however familiar, no longer connects me to the farms, to the neighbouring villages. Around the August orchard motionless in the motionless night, the countryside is slightly covered with fog, a dream enveloping an island embalmed in moonlight. Not the slightest wind between these stonewalls that would dispel the steady heat. Above my head, the slowly ripened clouds are opening like pieces of fruit.

For the Others

Here where no one speaks. In a bedroom perhaps, but I
no longer remember. The tree with its newborn leaves,
right next to me, at my level, is stirring. So many other
trees coming into leaf, and I don't know the last word.
The accord is in the silence, this slight wind. So many
other places as well. I am in the bedroom and outside the
bedroom. In the sunlight. In the joy I am seeking.

. . . More exactly, he is revolving around . . . , verb without an object; he is not revolving around something, nor even around anything; the centre is no longer the motionless sting, a point secretly opening the space in which one can walk forward. He who has gone astray is moving forward and remains at the same spot, wearing himself out by approaching, neither walking, nor standing still . . .

. . . A great silence is taking possession, all around me, of this place in which I dwell and it is as if all abolished distance were restoring me to a true distance . . .

ABSTRACTED FROM TIME

Fantasies by Way of Märchenbilder

Ein Märchen ist wie ein Traumbild,
ohne Zusammenhang.

A fairy tale is like a dream image,
without coherence.

Novalis

A Shadow, a Negative of the Sun . . .

A shadow, a negative of the sun surrounds the mountain summit that the child (does he know this?), long underway, perhaps will never reach.

His solitude, his surging forward.

Fever stirs him, though he doesn't hurry. Oh, his springy gait! His disproportionate vision!

The only promise, the only fire, is the beaming tutelary light that encircles him (oh, his springy steps!), that stays with him.

*

Invisible, slipping away, is the threshold of the night that he would definitely cross.

(Every now and then, the same hooting.)

Caught up in the action, whether he speeds up or not, he doesn't plunge into the thick spruce forest whose edge, as he progresses, withdraws.

So resolute (and if he were cut down in one blow?); so young (he won't flag), having ventured out with no idea of coming back. Whether he knows so or not, he has no chance of succeeding.

*

(Primeval.)

Bare, crepuscular, almost wholly visible now except for a lingering hood of mist and haze, the mountain rises immemorial, grows.

(Primeval, hooting.)

Memory, Scattered Mirror . . .

Memory, scattered mirror.

The water, the ground, the very island like azure haze.

The daylight in the high foliage interlaces its arabesques of fluty, ever-shriller, aerial voices.

*

Withdrawing into the clearing around the old bandstand.

Young mothers, the same ones as two hundred years ago, the very same ones, would have stayed to converse beneath the tall trees.

. . . once upon a time—summers that come back to vanquish the solitude, mixing memories, and nursery rhymes, and reveries—was once upon a time *below the young elms* becoming green again with every humming . . .

A place for festivities: Ah! the sweet tears fallen on this ground already enveloped, among confidante-like shadows, by the wing of the evening.

At night, around the old bandstand suddenly saved from ruin, the last visitors having left by the last boat, rounds and dancing blossom again.

Silent bandstand.

Back then was . . .

*

. . . your voice, the intimate network that your voice, more than words, will maternally have woven.

Bumping Along, but Gently . . .

Bumping along, but gently, the approach will be musical!

A stone struck on the clear and sonorous path (illusory repossession of the lands!) disturbs the order of the place.

Silently rising from the obscure depths, distinct, motionless, in correspondence (double shore, double expanse), trees, sky, spruces and pines are shining in the slumbering waters.

Pond that the briar borders with a braid of embers, dark backside of the day emptied, from below, of its light.

Unanimated splendour.

*

Where the blade of a cloud is nicked (the most furtive, the briefest wriggling at best glimpsed), a lightning flash, barely out of the water, vanishes.

Not any more—O panic! O peace!—would a swirl, a cry, arouse an echo.

A Tidal Wave . . .

A tidal wave. A flaring fire, a furore from far away passed on.

Behind my back (but this big room without lighting, perhaps deserted, a movie theatre, a dark cinema?), may its arrogance, its haughtiness, give itself free rein . . .

All of a sudden, like a top, I spin around, not at all to a face: featureless, bloated with smugness, scorn itself personified.

The incredible hurricane for once unleashed (a flaring fire)! Joy, blazing (a tidal wave)!

All of a sudden, to see him spread out between two rows of seats, collapsed there, sordid, neck in shreds, crushed, and the others standing in a circle, dumbfounded . . .

At last!

*

Outside, the next moment, abruptly.

Outside, a few yards from there.

Nothing in this interval, no, nothing.

From one tree to the next on the boulevard already over-whelmed by the heat of a May day (to surge back up? Never was . . .), among the thousand pennants of the foliage, blackbirds are chirping away.

A Remote Greeting . . .

A remote greeting in a lightning flash of joy, among these, those who with the same momentum were sharing the same expectation.

(That other one, however . . .)

The subsequent regret—yours, mine—of not having found a way to walk in concert.

(That other one almost at the same instant, without our yet knowing so, snatched away from us.)

Ultimately, each will have traced alone, from street to street, a sentence that the rain was washing away in turn.

*

May we once again be invited, for a moment, into the circle, the enclave where light has surged from shadow.

One more moment, warmed up by our presence (but him?), calmed down, (him, closed lips), may the gods, without being jealous of us, come to stand discreetly among us.

Borne along—them, us—by the silence, the incandescence maintained by the string instruments with their sisterly voices gathered together, unified.

Immortals bathed in serenity—like us, thanks to them, for a moment.

*

But him, still among us yesterday, around which faded music, which fire without heat for us, will he have joined *the greatest number*?

Henceforth a stranger, lost, absolutely lost.

*

In reunion with those, these together borne all the way to the sublime.

Soon separated at the intersection of nameless streets disappearing, dark and deserted, into the winter rains, the maze of the night.

Less Excess Brightness . . .

Less excess brightness (midday through the foliage), an effervescence circulating in the air is maintained.

At the heart of the beech woods as on a public square (clearing like a traffic circle, an esplanade, a cluster of trees in this barren spot), a grouping in not-too-orderly fashion.

No longer the time, the place to speak, to call out to each other loudly: these boughs, only, to respond to the slightest breath.

*

Alone in the crowd, haloed, margin of daylight, by the clearing.

Like a hermit forgetful of himself ('What have you come to look for?'); quiet (but, in the air, an effervescence, however light), unburdened of the weight of dreams.

A hermit, a wise man (teaching no lesson, however).

*

Like bits of wind, the shadow gradually crumbles.

With no speech, no voice; nothing but light.

Did You Dwell There?

Did you dwell there?

Bare, distinct.

Sonorous, but from noises coming, ever diminishing, from outside.

*

Led, guided through which hallways, over which itinerary, ultimately up which secret staircase that can be climbed only by groping my way?

Have reached the terrace that looks out on everything under the stars . . .

(Wouldn't those glimmers on the pond, pursuing me, instead be vertigo?)

Here I am under the stars next to you.

Once again (the absence however, the envelope of the absence), we would meet up with each other, free in an outdoors also free.

The brisk air, the sharp air; the pendulum of the air.

*

Far away . . .

Did you dwell there?

Far away the marshes become haze.

Luminous fringes of another night.

Darker . . .

Darker, the forest, the clearing beneath the weight of the sky and rashly crossed by railroad tracks.

And we, joyous, led from ambush to ambush all the way to these signs of a secret passing (were we making it up?), at night, all alone.

In the gloomy, unsafe (we wished it to be so) reaches where we played, near an embankment used as a garbage dump, quite simply, on the ground, a mattress saved from the sludge.

Beneath a kind of vault dating from the war (the other war, before our time, from another time that kept crumbling into ours), destitution and helplessness had made a stop.

Mothers, O maternal guardianship!

*

Runaway. Prowler. Tramp. Living in hiding or, having seen it all, a hermit.

Perhaps he never haunted these parts.

Or, all the way to the impossible (delirium and disappointments), what ardour had pushed him far from home?

*

Smoke! And already the bitter crepuscular disappointment.

Already, ruthlessly, shortened days; already time—ours, on our scale—comes undone, is diluted, dissolved into everyone else's.

The only thing left was to withdraw towards a village, towards homes without disorder, without turmoil.

Bitter and sweet effusiveness of the return!

A Scream Pierced...

A scream pierced our sleep, joined by stammering perhaps tempered, perhaps encouraged by our questions, our soothing words, just as soon.

... a blind eye? An outcrop in the clouds? Covered with ice? And swaying? Say ... A faceted mirror, but where?

A splendid vision, perhaps, or gestation monstrously brought to a halt.

Already, his lips pursed, already elsewhere, again grasped by his confusion (were we present?), already, in hebetude or rapture, he sinks into himself.

*

In silence once again complete, continues, unceasing, a scream which, deep inside oneself, each of us now doubts having heard.

And each of us secretly doubts whether, when his turn, his time, came, he saw that eye, that foamy reef, that moonstone like a star in the depths of night.

Moving Forward with an Even Step . . .

Moving forward with an even step, enveloped, borne along—by the forest no more than by the night.

Unless vainly, once there . . .

With an even step in the even (not truly trampled) shadow, any thought of an itinerary is dismissed.

*

The evening itself is taken apart, with a slighter movement, all over, in whole pieces, is crumbled by a dull paleness.

As if boles and foliage were going to be swept away, all chocks removed, in an imperceptible landslide.

Figure that is never finished; encounter that takes on no shape.

. . . flickers, motionless, a dull paleness, liquid twilight gap.

*

Is it the haze, is it the soil slipping away silently?

Perhaps a night path being repaved with stone?

Unless, each footstep effacing its own track . . .

Meanders and Undulations . . .

Meanders and undulations, from echo to echo, silently,
every word lapped up by the milky, aerial, bluish night.

Night, an end of night, yet (if the thread doesn't break)
still ours, entirely (our bodies each to each, with the same
elan), future, to come.

With the same momentum, marvel, renewal!

*

Ardent, awaited, delighted, you come closer—or perhaps
. . . no, so vivid is the hope, so total—riding on a byway
you have ridden up and down a thousand times, almost
with your eyes closed.

Without light, without noise (no glimmer even reflected
by the spokes, the wheels of the bicycle), you slip into the
milky night, merging with it.

*

. . . snaking, hugging the slope, the curve of the hills, of
the meanders and undulations, lingering in the combes,
the ravines, the level spots, volutes, caresses.

Chest, yours, rising and falling, happy, calmed down—

Farewell . . .

The plain, all the countryside and already, in the sky, the
first gleams.

Farewell.

*

. . . every word lapped up, at the top of the sky, tender,
ever tender to each other.

Fleeing . . .

Fleeing.

Snow, flame.

Fleeing in every direction over the opaque water.

A thousand glimmers, collisions, touches.

Farther on becomes a lantern again, wobbling, wavering; straggler on the other shore attached to my steps.

Who, following the edge of the night, as if returning from an unknown feast, would walk along, would stop, merely as I please.

Chimerical. Capricious. Distraught.

Lunar, despite the broad daylight.

Sweating . . .

Sweating.

(Sounds hollow.)

Abruptly, on what sign?

(Sounds hollow, washed-up conch.)

*

Between what walls? In what night? What hotel, from its rooms to its public areas cleaned out in the wink of an eye?

To bump, from the inside, so violently against the walls of silence!

Thrown deep into a vast bed whose sheets chill him, he comes to, without a thought, without energy, is brought back to life.

Absolute solitude.

*

Which is, with its shutters closed, but a former hot-spring establishment, shut down, vacant, lost in the mountains.

Rushing water, endless cliffs.

Around this man who has not found enough energy to move, shadows are building up.

Night, its immensity.

Slowly (washed-up conch), he sinks into absence, the din of the rapids.

As If, Delighted . . .

As if, delighted with the first warm weather (as a greeting, in waves, whiffs of unequal intensity, the scent of acacia), as if the very day were flowing into a meadow overgrown with daisies—sage.

Dew gleaming in flashes here and there.

Where dimples were deepening, where an imperceptible wind was leaving traces, the grass is already straightening up.

Fragrance. Winding footpath, effaced.

*

Or, instead (yet this perfume, this whiteness, in clusters), or, instead, floating on the surface of the water, undone, partly sunk, is a garland of daisies that the blue stalks of the sage would no longer bind.

*

. . . captive of the shadowy swirls of her love, the scarves of which could only suffocate her.

Bare Mountains . . .

Bare mountains.

The marble stone of dawn.

All the way to the transparent horizon, mountains and valleys overlap.

*

Nothing.

(The same shock, once the eyelids close.)

Is neither Delphi, nor Agrigento, nor any place trod on by the foot of an immortal.

Nothing but a kind of music, a fragrance.

*

Now, nearby, rises (is recognized?), on the hillside, the big stone house where a rest will be taken.

Now, familiar? House fallen asleep . . .

Grey in the shade of the northern side.

Guest house.

Already the front steps liven up with the first comings and goings.

In the frayed flax fibre of the night, blunt-arrowed voices vaguely mingle.

*

Dawn, the expanse!

Upon his gesture, apt (founding friendship) to populate the most arid solitudes, from the beginning, as brothers, from this very moment onward . . .

(In all times: won't he have obtained through poems, just poems—Oh! repatriation, and *it's poetic justice*!—the revelation of what he sees?)

After a long night-time journey, at first, upon his gesture (the triumphant transparency of the horizon), I turn around and give in to bedazzlement.

Before our eyes, the entire day unfolds piece by piece.

From the end of the expanse rises all the way up to us the vesperal valley in which a slow luminous river opens out, forks, flows together from meander to meander.

*

Surprise! Fulfilment!

From the sea, against the current (who from here would know how to say it? who would see it?), the water flows back up to its source, towards us.

THE BLACK OF SUMMER

Once Again, Absent

Puffs of wind are bringing her dwindled, almost faded (*like blueness, as at the end of an afternoon*) whiffs of wisteria. Balminess, mugginess are overwhelming her.

Dreamy, at the window; both her thoughts and her gaze vanish into the distance—no, they keep coming and going, running over rolling hills opening out onto the soft slopes before her eyes.
Or rather, once again, she is absent, borne along on a blanket of light . . .

*

She sees herself (*truer!*), she is walking lightly, melodiously (*quicker!*) within the colours of April, lending her voice, her tears.

Her walk: wakening within the complicity of the grasses, the stones to the wayside.
Her gaze: as she passes, a quivering in the thicket.
And her breathing: peaceful, yet steady, sometimes almost panting in the shadowy hollows; ever in unison with the slack, unmoving hour when her desires are ultimately diluted.
In the same way the sky, now and then darkening, starts to clear.

Her desires. The pollen of her desires like a brief colouration of the air.

*

Deliverance! At last a sob surges forth from inside her.
Once again it diminishes (*languor*!), dries up inside her; bursts out no more than the storm that has moved on behind the chimerical horizon.

Now all she has to do is yield to the languor, to the gloomy indolence of evening.

Voices and Cowbells

Low- to high-pitched sound hems (*delicious approach*) the octave bearing them along, all their weariness forgotten, towards what they would not wish to call awakening.

From far away within the dark yet limpid mountains: an echo.

Taking a footstep. Taking another, then another, regulating the heart. The whole sky smiles at them up there, where they are hiking.

Moving forward like this, imagining themselves moving across the vast expanses above the high pastures. They are barely rumpling the grass or, distractedly, tripping over a stone here and there.

Within the vast silk of twilight that is so palpable, so tangible, voices and cowbells are reverberating all the way to them despite the forest-covered depths; every now and again the voices and cowbells in the mountains bear them along like a rowboat in swelling waves.

*

Might the voices and cowbells grow weaker? This dread (*later*) of the moment (*later*) when, on the violin strings, the rising echo will fade away and the rostrums of the night will approach.

Out of reach, higher up, the elation of the stony slopes.

The Birth of Uneasiness

What he thought he was heading for when he hit the road (*the summer, the beautiful carefree summer*), opposing forces slyly draw further away from him in order to stultify him all the more—harmful, gruelling forces even more invincible than the raging wind. Still ahead of him the same distance he has not yet covered.

Childhood irremediably wounded by this first crack through which infiltrates the plague of solitude.

The places, although the same, as they ever have been (*how have they been marred so quickly?*), and time, all bear the invisible mark of this. Will keep it.

No help, no attraction, anywhere.

Futile inevitably (*where to go?*), taking a spin (*what's the use?*) becomes ever more of a burden as if, instead of moving forward, suddenly he were miserable, moving backwards.

*

Now he's thrown himself down against the embankment, listless, exhausted, the victim of an inner breakdown (*the strange uneasiness*) into which come falling the bicycle, the road, the sky, and the earth all bathed in sunlight.

May the devil take the meandering stream along which grew March marigolds joyously plucked, back then, despite their friable stems! In the cressets of the water, the affectionate maternal radiance helplessly drowns without a sparkle.

In his despondency, he is now far from hoping that such stagnant heavy gloominess (*the strangeness, the unknown uneasiness*) will ever lift.

A deserted memory (*the summer nonetheless, as it unfolds*) henceforth reigns over a sullen expanse, over land suddenly emptied of its sap.

Leaning against the embankment, the bicycle is resting lamentably at the edge of a road no longer leading anywhere.

On Charles Bridge

With that distraught look, that absent look of those for whom light no longer exists (a face, despite its youthfulness, that bears no fixed expression), noticing nothing of us or of all the beauty in our midst (*that slow poison that deliciously intoxicates the heart*), without being dazzled (*may the distinction between day and night never fade*), she probes with her stick the space in front of her (*emptiness, ah! emptiness around her as she passes!*), goes straight up the middle of the bridge towards the sunset: the last ray that the sun, like someone taking back his ante, would claim.

Amid the transparency where domes and steeples were hovering imperceptibly, amid the tender awakening of the vegetation, suddenly: Which peace to savour?

Earth and sky—all the beauty in our midst (*for the rest of us, all of us*), now tarnished and undeserved—has lost its sheen. How to make it gleam again? Sadness and nostalgia rolling in the now-darkened waters of the Vltava will provide no help. But blackened by the centuries and about to be devoured by the Prague night, would these saintly men and women in stone perhaps stake out a double hedge for this disinherited woman (*emptiness, emptiness all around her!*), for this solitary blind woman, from one end of the bridge to the other?

Mirroring their torments, their grace, her face could only have brightened for whomever would have been inclined to approach her.

Night-Time, A Same Night

Night-time (*a secret point touched in depth*), a same night, night-time opens out as much as the egret-bearing silence. They have barely begun to come together and a sumptuous tumult sweeps in, responding to a common thirst.

[Remembering this, what else does he do now but exalt it?]

*

Futile, any struggle to curb the rising, invading waters, although chimerical (*if he had known . . .*); and to wish to escape from games where mirrors keep multiplying themselves? From human being to human being (*from her to him*; actually, *from whom to whom?*), from a word, from a gesture surges forth an accord as if from glaring discord.

From yesterday to today, happy hustling and bustling as if everything were going to topple over into emptiness. Words (*their banality*) for unweaving and that once bound (*futile safeguards*), would bind again, perhaps.

Doesn't there seem to be a demon—detested, relentlessly pursuing his prey, of course—inside him, flopping around like a carp, the thief of the very thing (*fire*, *life*) that time has taken from him, that he will never receive from the Other (*the song will remain*) by whom he can only feel swindled?

*

Arc powerless to join them together, in their momentum towards each other; song deprived of the keystone.

Time Expanded

In the half-light of the room assailed by summer fires (*July again with its foliage, its almost colourless skies*), time expands.

Out of this world, in a place no longer containing us.

Self-enclosed (*around it, stupor and dismay*), this face that will never age, never know the ravages of time, keeps withdrawing, moving away, unaltered (*in its paleness, no shadow to darken it*), already fallen prey to the abyss.

Forever removed from our benevolence.

Henceforth upon us the weight of what will never have been said or exchanged, future continuous.

*

Time suddenly shakes up our bearings . . .

Back in place again, in the gaping emptiness into which we have been thrown, in the shadows of another room, the true to life portrait lost today (*its youth upstream from us*) of a grandmother's wrinkleless face.

A childhood home once stood joyous, white with the whiteness of summer.

*

Doubly dear (*the eldest of our elders back then*), may this face—closed to the blueness of summer filtering between the slats of the blinds—gleam in the half-light in which we have been left.

True to life (*whether today or yesterday*); immemorial. Our good, our own ruin.

Noon Fanfares

Are there two of us
or am I solitary
Paul Éluard

Everything, right now!

Dizzying obsession with joy (*choirs and brass instruments of May*) until it turns into the ritornello of anguish.

*

For the time being, breathtaking chilliness and transparency.

To go, over random paths, like someone on the lookout for an echo, through the forest assailed by a thousand flame tips.

These flying sparks! These songs blended with the eddies of solemn fleeting waters! These sparkles! These trills, a lofty turnstile whose streamers unfurl on treetops!

Headed off like me onto forest roads, into other places perhaps (*my breathing nonetheless to the same rhythm as his*), who is this Other also prey to impatience, whose pulse I can all but hear beating?

*

Today's elation! Ah, on the lips of the wind (*deadnettle leaves and labials*), mumbling on and on!

Getting through shadow! These cold zones between two fits of tenderness, and these hot flashes during a solitary hike—simple and dual—that is fervent, unbridled, unaware of the goal!

May this hike neither end nor my thirst be quenched as long as (*noon and its fanfares everywhere in the foliage*), as long as all promises have not been kept.

*

The Other, the unknown man—or woman—he who I was perhaps, our paths stone-paved once again with the help of the same words.

Fatality of Water

beyond the *Märchenbilder*

I

Unique, ultimate, an instant, a sound, dark gleam, whole, growing.

Ultimate, absolute, but an instant: he is embraced by the river, which he wants for himself (*'mine!'*), entirely (*'may your breathing be mine!'*), forever engulfed in its tumult.

The sounds (*'ah, the forces are everywhere unleashed against me!'*), all the sounds, are blended by the scarf of the river into a single scream carried beyond itself.

Words (*'Malediction, oh my burning reason!'*) and thought killed before they are born, crushed (*dizziness and deafening roar*) by the vice gripping him.

II

Such rage, such impatience for happiness!
Too late!

Held up by those who have carried him back to the shore, he stumbles in the street, holding his face between his hands, walled up (*his insanity*) in a scream never heard.

Do they know (*and his loved ones? especially she who runs up to him?*), do they know he will never return to them, now that he has become the mortal remains of himself?

Shattered: this extreme point reached.

Wasted, worn out (*fatality of water*), vacant minded (*what do we know about that?*), will he no longer even hear in the depths of his self the alarming cry '*I am lost*'?

April

Young, walking down the narrow jetty of the morning in the tender April light. So young (*nascent*), as if arriving from the wide sea by water that will never be seen so clear again. Emerging from no depths; as evidence (*childhood, all of childhood*), her gaze that nothing darkens.

Sister of pollens and inflorescences—promises, foliage tenderly growing green again, the freshness before speaking, before the budding of words—she moves towards the willows, on the shore, stirred by a spring-like coming and going.

Summer, will you follow in the footsteps of your messenger who keeps walking bare armed and barelegged despite the lasting cold? Child (*all of childhood once again*): a lightning bolt streaking through the day without tearing it; an explosion of colour, like the fragrance of gillyflowers.

For sure, she couldn't care less about the rags and tatters of the past season, but how ('*Schade*') not pay tribute to the new, beautiful season within her?

Sister of buds, of blossoming cherry trees; so young, ahead of herself, future, an instant at my level (*but the language*: '*Schade, ich verstehe nicht . . .* '), foreign, already on the shore at the heart of the refoliation—bud, inflorescence, herself a cherry tree . . .

The Black of Summer

Lost that joy gone off with the laughs, those voices more and more remote, indistinct, ultimately silent.

The acrid gruel of the night has thickened, drowning the minutes, the hours.

Like one who has watched shutters being closed, window after window, he is here, beneath the tall trees, sunk into silence, abandonment.

All around him the abode of shadows, the black of summer, has closed him in.

Ember after ember going out, strange appeasement, the last gleams of the feast.

An exquisite, secret mildness embraces him, detains him, after the others have left, near a dying fire that the high foliage has, already, almost stopped protecting from the rain.

And the clearing now: an impalpable wall.

*

In his veins runs darkly, strangely heavy, an indefinite time.

His sadness, his feeling of helplessness, down to the dregs . . .

These Armfuls of Sparks, These Embers

Poppies, again—denying solitude, traces of a fire about to flare up again, butterflies with folded wings stirred by the slightest wind, its craze for speaking unappeased, coming from the sea.

Together for once (*impossible*) in the middle of fields where so many sepulchres were dug: a greeting, on our carefree lips, to these armfuls of sparks, these scattered embers among the dry grasses!

So close our mouths were then, also ablaze . . .

*

To have a full share of space (*the azure, all the way to transparency*), of all space livened by July (*its ochre hues reflected back underground*).

Around them for an instant as they are sitting side by side sheltered from the heat, between them (*no matter how close they were*), for them alone sparkles the present while the stridency of the swallows scissors the air above their heads.

At the bottom of the hypogea, birds as well—colour, their flight! colour, their one song!—traverse the night.
(

Here, renewal.

Ephemeral, like a powder trail, like a flood of words to come, the same ochre, secretly, the same purple trembling (*their youth, forever*) troubles their heart.
So close (*impossible*) for the moment. May they be so. May they remain so.

*

Now that their time has come, it's up to others, happy, suddenly enriched by such a remote past, up to others to follow for a while, as if it were their own trail, this line of dots among the grasses in the suspense of the day, scarlet above empty graves.

. . . At this very moment already unaccomplished, burning.

Tangible Reality

At this hour of the afternoon, making a stop at some distance from the town on which, incidentally, the curtain of rainstorm, obliquely drawn to the side, is falling.

Over there, the whole shadow of the sky (*elsewhere, the sun is now shining*) is gliding along as if across an immense imaginary roof.

Appeasement, rest, at the top of the only hillock dominating this expanse where, over a swirl of hedge-bordered fields, nothing hinders sight.

Near the three trees, making a stop at the heart of reality and turning towards the west, in full daylight (*almost a veil of heat, a kind of shimmering*), at this place spotted from afar and finally reached, a point of solitude much more than a point of view.

*

More important than the trees with their dense foliage is the halo of clarity hovering around them, regardless, while at their feet evening is already piling up down the slope. Will the halo welcome in some vagabond or idler when night comes, after the departure of children vaguely busy fishing (*their shouting behind my back, their vexed cries at every unsuccessful cast*), the edge of the pond then swarming with shadows?

*

Houses, watermills, pasturelands fade from one part of the perspective to the next, plot after plot of land keep dwindling to flee ad infinitum and thoughts left blank scatter, free as the air, into the wider space of the sunnier weather.

Tangible reality—fabulous, imaginary.

WITHIN THE VOICE'S REACH

The Bird Sharply Winging

Sharply slicing its wings through the narrowest spot
of the gorge as if, emerging from shadows, a hand were
giving—yet in emptiness—big scissor cuts.

The fine jumble of waterfalls, whirlpools, eddies, folds
and refolds, sheaves of foam that it flies through without
veering!

Will it join one shore of the night to the other one? In
any case without putting things in order or drawing up a
reliable boundary. Having grazed the water, it will not
blacken it, this messenger of oblivion.

Renewal of Looking

First colouration of dawn, intimate, skin-deep. First expected, promised, caresses.
Suddenly the explosion.

Reeds, aviary of the day.

Or Laurel

Wintry (*its hues: in the mouth their flavour, discreet, or laurel*), is it the mountain which, lightened, little by little rises?
Or the first blushes of morning.

Already being diluted in the faraway dream.

Joyous, Ascending

As if penetrating all the way to here, having seeped between the slats of the fog (*promise, rip*), and everything is suddenly clearer, more spacious, larger.

Higher up, entry into broad daylight: mine the winter still uninhabited (*a bare room*) and the expanse seemingly unfurled by a single gesture.

Fresh on the fresh snow rebounds—freshness—the voice of a child out of sight.

From nowhere, joyous, rising, the voice is inflexed (*pure morning inflection*), follows the curve of the combe, slowly coming back up from the shadow.

Without Ruts

Enough to stumble over an invisible stone, or a tree root,
below the silent baptismal snow levelling out the path,
spreading over it, imperceptibly lifting from the earth the
undergrowth, relieved of the burden of night.

An Unequal Footstep

The border of the shadow followed on this side where the cold has dug its ruts, with an unequal footstep like someone afraid of getting caught up in the fringes. Almost within hand's reach, the sun, from the other side, comes to ruffle up the edge.

There where, with unpursed lips, no voice . . .

In between, in the clearing, the bare earth is like light with smothered sparkles, lumpy because of drought, uncrossable.

Cannot Come Back from It

By dint of brutally pulling in opposite directions on the night (*already?*), the thick night (*no, no, not yet!*), they end up bursting its seams apart.

Cawing sounds filthy with sleep.

Their turbulence (*enough!*) and, owing to wider and wider rips, their ceaseless comings and goings (*I can't stand their sight, they hurt my eardrums*), no chance now that this will be put to rights.

Ever in the Present

Having become silent—since when?—birdsongs would crumble, shattering on the stony trail sticking out from under the snow and frost.

Deep in the chest, enough to take one's breath away, the stars of the cold are wavering.

For the Moment

You grebes and coots blowing with neither rhyme nor reason into your elderberry blowpipes, briefly, intermittently (*a sound*, *a call*, *a sign*), here, there, unforeseeably, ever elsewhere, how many of you are there like this, out of sight, untying in a snap armfuls of reeds?

We who have long been listening have no duty, for the moment, other than applying ourselves to not losing the thread.

Places Now Different

Touched by a gaze, in the distance light up, clearing and roads, or the fork of a stream, vague traces of snow.

Places stripped of their names (*at last! at last!*) and now different, scattering themselves at the end of the afternoon.

All the way to the high clouds, in the mirrors of the sunset, all the way to the barriers of the wind is lengthened and reflected, from one hovering point to the next, a powder trail.

Multicoloured Spinning Top

A moment, a calling out left without an answer (*what does it matter?*), a voice cast towards the sun and somewhat hesitant in the empty light (*uninhabited light*) echoes (*all the sparkling of youth*), shines down the street it has just liberated from boredom, is soon swallowed up by the wan motionlessness of March.

Multicoloured spinning top, happy with a trifle, surge forth again!

Perhaps underground it keeps moving towards a suddenly less-improbable spring.

Frantic Retreat

Fleeing (*the irresistible thrust!*) while crowding together, jostling each other along the shore, and spattered by the waves splashing up again.

Like—defeat (*poles and pennants pestered by the wind*)— an armed gang, a troop from a past century beating a retreat, with no strength left, under enemy fire.

Saxifrage Cherry Tree

Greetings to the smallest wild cherry tree surging forth from the wall, at eye level, between two coping stones! It could all but (*gloriously!*) go unnoticed, barren and scorned, living off nothing, fervent, austere.

Gloriously because of its minute, barely blossomed flowers!

The bees pay no attention to it, nor does the magpie walking along the wall. May the weeders (*its modesty*) do the same!

Fermata

Impossible to stop looking at, to move away from in the least, the last, lost, flickering piece of daily debris piercing the haze.

From here, hardly a pinhead.

This slight luminous point is fading out little by little, a deceptive landmark soon absorbed in the drifting, the drowsiness of space—squeezed back together? expanded?—where all distances are nullified.

Weather Clearing Up, April

Clearness, the same clearness suddenly shining every-
where.

Clearness seemingly letting herself be carried away with
regret, sliding along languidly, joyously, cheerfully, lin-
gering in hugs and kisses, in love with herself, scattering
her reflections that fragment as soon as they are gath-
ered; soon she dives headlong into the rapids, emerging
with each lash of the water, impatient for the heights of
pleasure.

Or this: a foliage of droplets suspended below a large
glass rooftop just now freed of its canvas canopy.

Moveable Mirror

Extreme clearness of the daylight, a jubilation (*its fresh-ness*), a morning water gushing forth, gushing forth again, indefinitely stumbling and catching herself, losing her footing and then rebounding up to the summit of her song.

Her pirouettes: a sonorous fluttering that would crown a spurting fountain with a moveable mirror.

Which, towards noon, interrupted (*mute equilibrium point*), will no longer have to stand up to the wind.

See you tomorrow, warbler, you frivolous companion who has stayed out of sight in the trees.

Amid the Persistent Clearness

Unhurriedly, on the esplanade, the evening is hanging out its linen here and there, on the ground between the trees, from moment to moment (*ah*! *the slowing down of passing time*!) putting off nightfall.

In the distance rises the narrow yellow-stoned facade whose top vanishes in the clumps of shadow.

To hover in between, in this persistent clearness, carried along by the fragrance of the lime trees.

Double Sky

There, where great momentums of vegetation raise a hedge of chirping that favours (*and the rustling of wings*) the circulation of the light.

Beyond, in equilibrium within the suspense of time and the spacious immobility (*my breathing*: *come up for air and dive again*), two skies, two expanses of water, two ponds of clouds.

The Diaphanous Shadow

Her chest barely quivering, as if she were going to come to (*no, however*); her lips barely moving, sky or water, bearing the dawn.

Diminished, the shadow is brightening, livening; noise of a scattered scintillation.

Breathing softly, smiling, happy in her light sleep, wave after wave (*murmur fading away*), her dream is cradling her all the way to the heart of the reedy marsh along the lake.

Amorous instability.

Towpath

On the unsteady, uneven, badly cemented stones of a structure held together by means of makeshift repairs, from moment to moment, almost with every step, to have to keep one's balance.

Boat-hauler of time, haul!

High Place

Yes to this musical unfurling of the vegetation, this explosion of chirpings scattering or intersecting in disorder and carefreeness.

To remain long stretched out lazily in the attic, touching the sky, daylight everywhere seeping in between the ill-jointed roof tiles.

These flashes merging light and voices are imperceptibly covered by the shadow once again become, almost entirely, sovereign.

Far

From the depths of the plain comes feebly (*one motor; soon another one*) noise from the almost deserted road at this hour, absorbed in its bends, nonchalantly following the stream, gently hugging the curve of a hill, letting itself be taken over by silence.

Still vague and faraway, reverberations of another rumbling.

Imperceptibly, almost imperceptibly as the light shifts (*only down there some dim glimmering*), idle, dawdling thoughts start moving in the slowness of the afternoon.

No haste, no troubling displacement except for a gloominess (*my meteorological instability*) suddenly ready to engulf everything.

The storm will perhaps soon be upon us.

At the Mouth of the Stream

Ever renewing herself, the stream glides by, making ribbons and fringes of light glide by, wave, whirl, ribbons and fringes carelessly and too-loosely stitched together by a duck couple streaking just above the water.

Old togs, frills and flounces, what's the use?

Now completely clear, the stream lets herself go, with seeming listlessness, mated to silence and, from one shore to the other, absentminded, lazily pulling the sheet of noon back over herself.

Unsure Footsteps

From afar can barely be heard the noise of metallic crates or barrels (*the low notes, will they go up the scale?*) seemingly being jumbled along in a cart.

Or if, to shake up the greyness, little bells being jiggled in vain?

A thousand clashes (*waves and wind*), a thousand crashes, and another thousand, all the way to rapture!

Invisible Mountain

As to the darkness which, without warning, has thickened behind our backs: coming upon us (*let's turn around*) is the mountain itself, not the rain, covered with how many grey cottony envelopes like more or less thick moth-eaten shawls carelessly tossed over its shoulders?

One after another they tear apart (*let's turn around again*), laying bare a new, neat, luminous line without any hazy spots; they give a base back to the motionless traveller, the shadowy mountain.

Found again: the echo of other mountains (*us, our wandering*), after the downpour.

Within the Voice's Reach

Moving sky (*again*), upside down, turned greyish.

While gliding imperceptibly, unfolding, finding itself the same (*again and again*), cramped between its two banks where, from one to the other, it would be easy, so easy, to exchange a few words.

But which words, even the slightest ones, could cross the deep silence without sinking, the darkness of this water whose surface is left undisturbed by a slight ripple?

Upside down (*clouds or stones*), the streambed itself leads the current on.

Exuberant Stream

Here I am at a bend in the road, walking along a corn-field, exuberant stream; the sparkling, the blinking of its waters slowly, silently, luminously crumples and unfolds the gaze, offering it an extension.

Leaves brimming over. Their rustling, their shine.

Weak is the wind. Barely at my ears, a murmur of vowels.

Hut of Wind

Rickety hut randomly planted there by the wind, with no foundations, a rough assembly of salvaged boards painted white more or less, in a hurry, for the occasion.

Will burst into bits with the first projectile that falls.

Air, Water, Fire

Land narrowed by gloomy rain, fallen from heavy ledges.

. . . would narrow, were it not for the wind and, in its hachures, an oriflamme, luminously.

As the Crow Flies

Down there shines the sheet-metal roof of an isolated shed, perhaps abandoned, perhaps, for whomever would approach (*but the distance!*), unattractive, rusty, drab.

Wavers, gradually rises, seems to float to the beat of soothed breathing.

Your gaze, quick, focus it (*but the blurriness!*) before the target fades away in the flare of the twilight.

Ever a Stream, its Attributes

Softly, slowly (*her unconcern*), gliding regretfully from sleep, still half-dozing yet cheerful, joyful, already beaming, pretending to stretch, nevertheless soon sleeping late once again.

Smooth (*her youth*), relieved of her shadows. Her wrinkles, any frowns, fade away accordingly.

Wily (*from day to day, her appeal*), for the pleasure of it, not without languor, like moving one's tongue across one's lips, she skims and re-skims along her shores.

At a Distance

These laughs, the water of these laughs in the morning and these murmurs borne by the wind, however light, how to grow weary of them?

No words, however; at most, relentlessly, skipping, retreating and skipping on the pebbles.

Far out over the water, as far as one seeks to see, sky, lake, the submerged gaze loses all limits.

Blue almost evaporated. The summer in its transparency, the naked summer.

From the Same Belvedere Again

Villages and clouds, and the neighbouring hillsides, and the entangled fields and wheat, paths lazily linking farms, sheds, and the migratory roofs: taken up (*sun and scorching haze*) in the whirlwind of the summer, their arrangement blurs.

From the terrace overlooking the plain, to wait so long for the storm still absent, off-centre, touch-and-go, unpredictable, slipping between the pyramids of air.

Broad Daylight

Having reached the ridge of the combe, the sun withdraws even more.

In such a confusion of haze (*moving*, *at the edge*), the forest, itself subjected to pitching back and forth, would drift were it not, pillar of the east, here and there a scotch pine.

Vanished, the path (*in broad daylight*, *brilliantly*!), engulfed or almost by the influx, the flow of dead leaves that, at best, have left a wine-coloured trail; may it lead back to the faultless light of the morning!

Demarcation of the Uncertain

For what sharing this barely drawn, straight, never-veering line, this blind scissor cut given by a sure hand?

Lake, haze; any tearing?—none.

Perhaps no sailboat was. Perhaps did not happen.

On the Alert

Among the dead leaves that it stirs (*head and beak*), that it stabs, shakes, that it rips, that it turns over and pushes aside just as soon, rejecting sometimes whole little piles of them, what is this impatient one (*how feverish, black-bird, every jab of your beak*!), this busy one, ever on the alert, looking for?

What sentence? What former version of a poem (*the poem*), of a dream (*the dream*), carelessly put aside, lost, submerged among countless other drafts, perhaps never written?

By dint of variants, needless repetitions, he begins to believe in it, after so many fruitless attempts (*all this bother, this muddle-jumble of dead leaves*), he imagines it as ultimately being (*will he give up?*) the only one worthy of being kept, when, for that very reason, it cannot be found.

Passage

Ah! Leaving, as the crows heckle, the shade of the little spruce woods, having committed no other crime (*not at all: a bitter dispute between them, instead*) than passing through, discreetly.

Continue, crazy crows, to flap around the heavy forest curtains! As if, when the soot of the night invades, frantically beating one's wings will suffice for shaking it off!

All Slowness

Darkened, black by dint of being so deep down (*rock cliffs, spruce trees hemming her in*), barely moving water, smothered, faceless, almost lifeless, lying sick on the streambed, deprived of the future.

Will somewhat shine further on again (*once more, in broad daylight*), perked up, tying together shadows.

Memory Erased Proportionately

By heaps, rubbles, smudges, by sparkles, by masses, sun-like on the crack, relentlessly it pours out, dropping, sliding, slumping, bouncing back up, inexhaustibly feeding its fall. In vain, exulting, it furiously tries to shatter the daylight, to shatter itself, to ruin itself.

In the effervescence of noon, however, what spectacle is more joyous?

Memory erased proportionately, splendid.

Going Back Down the Path

As if (*so close now*), once the heights had been reached, recovering one's youth were at stake! Shutters open (*the tender whitecaps of the wind*), the sky widens and, wave after wave, crest after crest, space.

Now a level path; walking and breathing eased.

Return (*shadow and mugginess to chew over*) through the rainy, oppressive spruce forest, through the rotting tank of dead leaves sticking to the soles of shoes—and already the dulling din of the road, the laborious insistence of motors being driven hard up the combe.

Autumn Procession

Between shores strewn with confetti and other novelties, noiselessly, what light skiffs, seemingly ethereal, would be heading off, each donning its colours, each at its own pace?

In fact, as they crowd together, jostle each other while taking their places, they almost capsize.

Caught in eddies for a moment, vanquished, scattered, suddenly without dazzle, further on once again they disperse in the calmed down currents.

Larches

Edged with fine powder standing out against the clearing; a less tactile, vibratory screen for filtering the silence.

At these customs, a seemingly two-sided exchange, a ceaseless exchange of Sameness.

Animated by a mere point of colour.

To speak of openwork? Instead, of a fortunate crumbling of the light, lingering on the fingers of vegetation denying itself, effacing itself.

Vanishing, scattered by the chilly breeze barely grazing it.

Rain Musician

A mute harp, this light breeze softly blowing along the shore!

Mute despite the rain's fingertips touching all the strings at the same time.

Making the Crumbling My Own

Still whiteness, but dull beneath the lifeless sky, in this trail of clouds bent on gnawing the ridge of the mountain (*too close today, too burdensome*) like acid attacking, biting, the copper plate.

Or, very slowly infiltrating between the dog-eared tops of the spruce trees (*also dull, that black*), like a poison flowing down into the veins.

Devil-May-Care

Soon the feast! As if the facade had been whitewashed for the sunrise, yet carelessly (*the wind*), in a rush (*speed and torment*), devil-may-care.

Working blind; blind night snow.

Everywhere (*laughter or desolation*) uncovered gaps, repainting, lumps, thick spots, trickles. Pitifully, the filthiness of badly covered roughcast shows through.

Later, the greyness swept away: the brass instruments, all scintillation.

Voices to Come

The resonant tingling of the air this morning.

Crumbling of the cold: scattering, swirling (*armfuls of voices to come, if they could find a place to land, to gather*), miserly (*slighter handfuls of chilly wind*) and so light (*barely any dust*), these snow seeds suddenly come to a halt, recovering whiteness and transparency, all at once snatched upward.

Like notes from a violin that are happy to be scattered, to fade away at the most high-pitched limit.

Sun-like, in Splendour

Over this path now potholed, he will have gone (*sun-like, splendorous*) before me, a daytime messenger having hiked through the forest at the height of the cold and then vanished with it; he will have passed by unnoticed, too discreet, will have left behind, as a devotee of solitude, only the slightest trace among the heavy ruts of mud and mist carved out since then by the woodcutters and their machines: tracks showing lumps of snow, dull, gnawed-at pieces of ice (*the other day's snow*) chipped, rounded, as the foot strikes them.

Like pebbles or, as they are rolled insatiably across the tongue before being spit out again, the words of an impossible poem.

Making it Silent Again

All spots of colour pulverized, the millstone of shadow creaks while turning amid the dark pines, the blackness, the invisible.

Quarrelling jays: brutally jostling each other and streaking left and right until doors and windows are slammed shut as if out of anger. Each one squawking louder than the next until they grow hoarse, choking after shouting so much abuse.

At the bottom of the throat, a bitter taste of evening and wet, dirty, chewed snow.

Quarrelling Jays Again

The air that is invisibly, almost imperceptibly crumpled, on the other side of the hedge: the time for presents having come, it seems one is readying, ill masking its shine, to carefully remove something (*no less than the daylight*) from its bulky though lightweight packaging that is torn open, ripped off in pieces, set aside.

Perhaps a jay couple.

Their sudden squawking, like curses, their uncouthness, while they are busy, brutally bringing us back to chores, to down-to-earth concerns.

Stitched with White Thread

In the distance, lines and dotted lines emerge and just as quickly vanish, disappearing and reappearing every which way in the intensity of the blue.

Unscathed, however: its scope. Safe from any mending, cutting, or folding though roughly stitched with white thread ready to give way and neither sewing together nor patching anything to anything.

Unpredictable coming and going of seagulls at the end of the bay.
With a flap of their wings, they slip away, crossing the blue, moving from the inside to the outside; twirling, threading their way through emptiness again and again. Memory and emptiness.

Free as the Air

Morning: less wavering.

Barely pink, the daylight (*tenderness before any refoliation*), the daylight's hot-air balloon comes to a standstill amid the coolness.

Attached to nothing, holding on to nothing, hovering (*no longer touching the ground or seemingly so*), such, above our heads, are the trills of invisible birds.

While Walking Along

Stones.

Sisters of calcareous slabs surged up from underground and making the grassy ground bumpy here and there, stones worn out into a sheen, sticking out more or less, unequal in size, let me spell them out step by step while walking along.

On what syllables will my heels trip up? The sentence— ordinary, ever the same—seemingly rising, heads off in quest of meaning, unaware of the ending.

CUTS

Blurred Landscape

Winds rather than rain hachure sky and land.

Born of night, of the entanglement of night, tremulous, muddled and distinct (resurgence), a blurred landscape, a rough draft of a landscape, against the sunlight, refusing to be fixed, and as a result (a negative, a working photo) failing to attain colour. In the developer in which it should sink, a hand delicately stirs it.

Tempestuously, fine weather.

Though not staying put, the joy of feeling here, at home, in total turbulence.

Luminous effervescence tumbling down the hill in every direction, sweeping over hillsides and ravines, in disorderly fashion abundantly sweeping onward, black, yes (illuminating quality of black, clearer when viewed from farther away) stirring, crossing, scratching the paper with a thousand strokes as fine as spidery scrawls, or hairs—an ample head of hair tangled up and come undone.

In what is most intimate, fervent bustling.

Night or shadow bristling up, remodelling, re-undulating the land and lying low in its folds, its back-folds. Although caught up in the movement, the trees move, deliberately, no more than, on a hillside, a church or convent surmounted by a dome.

Redeployment of the daylight: barely will I have had time to grasp the frayed landscape or its double as it flies past in a hurry, to embrace it (all of a sudden, in its slightest details), greeting it with a broad gesture in passing as if to draw it into my own race.

Cuts

The unscarred sky

Pierre Reverdy

I

Out on the sea, a bare horizon; a strip of haze halfway up the slope of a mountain range; in the sky, a bar or bulge of clouds on the surface of the water: each time, a cut, even slight, an ephemeral single, double or multiple incision which, with borders absent, defines no line of demarcation, damages nothing. Trimmed or not, as if engraved by a steady hand with a burin, a gouge.

Watching with increased tension.

Shadow held in check by the dyke,
cut in the dusky light.

Will brim over.

Stream convoying the night.

Gleaming, it breathes:
wound soon effaced.

Like one
—water—daylight—
straight, steady, slender
crafted by a sharp edge.

All of a sudden, mirror shattered.

Line born of the wind.

(What buried brook
would it border—or embroider?)

Barrier, no barrage
narrow and shivering:
the snow, unbound everywhere,
does not know this.

(reeds lost in the wintery plain)

This advance:
a harp of reeds.

From ebb to flow
it barely stirs,
heading for the open sea.

In daylight,
without breaking it,
—its wake narrow—
goes.

Calls, responses
relayed from trill to trill
on its journey.

Boundary marking
forcefully, irritatingly,
jostled by the wind.

Beeches, perhaps sorbs
giving meter
to the undulating ridge.

Delightful these long,
short, unequal intervals.

Like, from so far away,
pricking one's ears.

Jagged mountain.

Keeping it apart from the sky,
drawn out, muddled up,
is a rip.

Its very base unstable.

Mountain again, split in two.

White, haze,
bandeau inherited from the night.

Like speech, severed.

Here
looking founders.

Down below,
russet colours everywhere licking the ground,
bristling it up a little.

Fire enclosed in its drowsiness.

The sunset redness
brightening
once past the shadowy zone.

So we would go back in time,
effacing one by one its wrinkles,
water, reflections bearing me along step by step.

Water, its monotony:
barely as if, in the least,
a border incises it.

Acuteness of the gaze.

From one shore to the other,
without deviating.

Falls,
falls on its back.

Exhausting undertow
which—and this

Which, as din,
long stays with me.

Stream
in its swirls
bearing voices.

All jumbled up,
ribbons of voices
gleeful, gloomy.

Gleeful.

Dull degenerated
stubble against the sunlight.

Its indistinct lines
minced by the evening.

Yet was in glory.

High foliage.

In dialogue,
at the slightest puff,
with the wind.

Speechless to my tongue.

II

'The unscarred sky', *continuously, such as during a mid-summer day when the light remains everywhere true to form, or perhaps only a mere moment is at stake, like a hand sliding across a smooth cloth without meeting up with any rough spots, any creases. Lightweight is the air, the foliage, the shadows.*

Almost as soon, 'Everything tears apart,' *at the bleeding crook of the horizon.*

The valley, the high places:
equally motionless
in the winter light.

(*after Chiyo-ni*)

Chalk flying like a seagull
lining up a gardener's string
along an invisible line.

Distinct abode,
bare screen,
the sky almost black.

High spots, low spots
like upstrokes and downstrokes
equally shared in the light.

Snow:
for an instant
its full sovereignty.

On high clustered trees parade,
their ranks serried,
blurring the view.

Vagaries of the hike.

Now nearby appears,
wide-eyed in broad daylight,
a clearing.

Doves,
downpour or column,
marching from west to east
on the horizon.

Spring migration.

Led along, the mountain
is also on the move.

(*cloudburst*)

The nice confusion—not at all!—
of gathers, flounces
puffing out over and over again.

From the same force emerge,
white heads stuck close together,
a thousand needle heads.

Soon all set, beaming,
—bright white, all shiny—
will see herself as a bride.

(hawthorn in May)

Once more,
to espouse in full flight
the wind.

Blazing up
a wisp of straw.

Heavy, weighted down,
feet do not leave the ground.

Shadow,
shadows of morning.

Lake:
mirror with stillborn glimmers.

Their singing exercises
strangled by the cold,
the return of the cold.

Forest like smothered fervour,
numbed.

Past, future
will soon again form a canopy
above us.

Showing, slightly,
rising from the combe
a veil of steam.

Soft soil.

Haze or mist
seized by the cold.

(first sign of the season to come)

At mid-slope
the fog,
—blanket, ocean—
peels off, blisters.

Almost,
with the foot,
grazing it.

Without a nick
gleams
the horizon's razor edge.

Mountain
weary of its slope.

Which, slowly, tumbles down.

At last stretches,
happy, flappy,
slouching, muzzle on the ground.

On the tip of the tongue,
as far as the eye can see.

As much mountains as clouds.

Luminously,
upside-down ocean.

As far as the horizon,
scratched at, roughed out,
unrolling its folds.

This high road
once again,
deserted, white.

These footsteps, these years,
mentally.

III

Vertically, gradually, in the calmness today of the beech grove, divisions and subdivisions widen and tighten the space around me. Gaps, openings (my respiration, easy), *do not look out, do not need to look out, on an elsewhere.*

High up (here and there, among the trunks, the ascending twists of an oak), *in vain, very high up, the treetops seemingly strive to reap the wind.*

Aerial sowing,
stuck in the immobility.

Diurnal stars
strewn over the ground.

Debris of night
crushed, white,
sieved.

Sparks of foam
shooting up from an inferno of snow.

Dust dropped down from the clouds.

Like superb shivering peacocks,
at the edge of the dead season,
a row of aspen.

Shadows scattered, all of them.

Above,
the sky is crumbling.

Trees or herds afar
disorganized
in the motionlessness of morning.

Waiting without impatience for the wind.

Light absorbed
from one curtain of foliage to the other.

Breaking, fractioning
increases.

Mirror, green water
down below
all the way to the darkness.

Brushwood or tree cluster.

Which,
from the buzzing light
rustles everywhere.

Winged forest.

Harsh, husky, hushed
noise of wings.

Go, come, in twos,
swish down
from one thicket to the next.

Like one crumpling
in the shade
brown wrapping paper.

(*amorous chasing*)

Flogged,
trounced by the windstorm,
rough, bare mountains
arch their backs.

Here,
battering into emptiness.

Afar,
a necklace of haze.

Around my head
a blindfold of coolness
hides my view of it.

Invisible threads,
tightened, relentlessly untightened
invisible.

From moment to moment
—brief, moving punctuation—
air, space recreate themselves.

Elasticity becomes mine.

(blackbirds and, further on, cuckoo)

Forest: from all sides,
endlessly, closing up on the hike,
ramparts with a thousand flowery narrows.

Immurement
yet with drafts rushing in.

Finely filtered,
the daylight liberates.

Effaced land.

Not far
—perhaps the shore—
floating in indistinctness
a bird-bank.

Will be restored,
later,
only partly.

Shivering, it sounds lightly shrill,
offbeat
to the caprice of time.

Will not go far.

For a moment,
has replaced the foliage
scattered by the wind.

(trees and bell tower in complicity with December)

Solar, this roof,
page onto which surges
the light, fascinated.

During the night appeared
blindly
snowy handwriting.

Poem in tatters.

Eyelids kept
tightly shut by the sun.

Substitute for any landscape.

The Slightest Unevenness of the Ground

Every inch of the way, the tattered shadow loses ground, keeps mounting as best it can, while retreating, the low dry-stone walls that are as unfit for containing it as for dividing the daylight restored fold by fold.

Mounds, bulges, gullies.

Would come to me, crested or not with tufts of yellowed grass, one lightly swelling, the other ready to flatten out, a wave, the next one, and the one after that.

Unfurling space, the slightest inflection, from one jump to another, the slightest unevenness of the ground, closely, very closely follows the proceedings of the heart or commands them; at the very least, says them.

The slightest stretching of clouds . . .

THE PROOF IS IN THE VOID

Cocoon

A book, a poem, like a cocoon into which one settles, but temporarily, fearing suffocation. A metamorphosis is needed.

Abyss

Destitute in front of a landscape, nonetheless seen and questioned a thousand times, having been unable (tension, exhaustion) to reduce myself to it: everything fled away at the very moment it revealed itself.

Could I have been blind until then to such dispossession, concerned only with beckoning to and finding words assuredly bearing life, yet without seeing that the poem (what I would like it to be) is born of what makes it impossible and, engulfed in duration, does not let itself be immobilized or captured?

An endless quest, not without an objective and bearing its own justification.

Art, Artifice

Pressing into a mould which should make any form explode. Poking among cold ashes instead of setting words on fire.

The Contents of Words

Impossible that the word is dissociated from the thing, that it does not respond to contents more or less well defined, more or less complex, conscious, subjective or, if need be, diverted from common usage (as in the Proustian 'to cattleya').

Being lost: ever this overriding impression of a few early childhood memories constantly enriched, modified by outside contents, from *Tom Thumb* to *A Balcony in the Forest*, by everything swept along by words, by sayings, in order to crystallize into an experience that is both commonplace and singular.

I am still chilled, or burned (was I three years old?) by the fright of no longer finding my way in a public establishment with dark hallways, probably, in reality, a labyrinth of relatively narrow dimensions, and where it is unthinkable that I would have been allowed to wander off more than a few steps.

Resemblance

Echoes, reminders, recognition, what is similar restores life, prevents attaining anything unique. Exile and refuge.

The Human Being

We have access to particular human beings, each considered in his individuality. However, what is singular,

unique (absolute?) most certainly eludes us. Our classi-
fications cannot pin it down, but we keep proceeding by
means of approximations (assuming we still consider
them to be so), seeking resemblances, filiations, while
labelling, lending (this is the right word) a character to
each and everyone.

Always moulds to save us from what is *formless*.

Distance

Coition. Tension towards an ultimate blob of solder, an
insanely brief intensity. The same trajectory and the same
tension during poetic contemplation, creativity. The same
craving, the same desire pushing towards an at-once pre-
cise and indefinite goal, the same sudden bursting out
(but not, indeed, the same outcome) and the same ambi-
guity of the Same and the Other. Momentum and fall.
Proximity and distancing, a single time.

Resemblance

Deceiving mirror of resemblance. Not if it is our only
truth.

Words, likewise: no neat primary meaning. Every
meaning is derived, secondary, perverted, figurative.
Etymology never goes back to the origin, by definition
out of reach (if need be, presumed).

Covering Over the Tracks

Edmond-Henri Crisinel:'Now you will perhaps better understand why I have been unable, up to now, to finish the first part [. . .]. I am still trying to "cover over my tracks."'

One covers over tracks in order not to be caught up with. Why, in writing, so much alteration, sterile redrafting, and trouble taken if it is not to keep burying ever-more deeply what gave flight to the poem, in order to forget it, obliterate it, though not annihilate it?

Below, Beyond

They are *them* and I am *me*. Outside and inside, the ego and others, painfully.

No more is designated than the trace of a rupture, a gap between terms themselves lacking content. Either an unbridgeable breach deepens or the threat of a violation of territory increases.

The Other

To define oneself only by means of the Other, the *not-I*—human beings and things; to come to life only in this way.

A poem is entirely momentum towards the Other, love, though it is but absence.

Labyrinth

The infinite in the finite, not beyond. The despair of getting out of this? Also the happiness (or bewitchment) of being unable to go all the way, *to see the end of it*, of moving among what is familiar yet also different, strange, unknown as much as known.

Here again will take place the confrontation with the monster who has remained invisible until the end—our end.

Childhood Impressions

Shall I go with them or not? In the bottom of my throat, so to speak, the acidic taste of such hesitations returns, until I feel sick: happiness and joy are there where I am not, with those whom I did not wish to follow, and there is still perhaps time to catch up with them.

(I see, a remote memory, my father and my sister moving away over a bumpy path; neither the presence of my mother with whom I thought I wanted to stay, nor the mildness of the afternoon, free me from the quagmires into which I sink.)

This or that: in any case, the severing has occurred, the charm is broken, irremediably.

Suicide

To take poetry as the equivalent of a death experience? Of a failed suicide attempt?

Fascinated by the blankness of the page, I mime my death, or try to believe it.

Absurd

The world is devoid of meaning. Mute, it calls for meaning to which responds our yearning for missing meaning. The quality of the responses doesn't matter (we will always be swindled), only that the abyss is closed up again.

Daily Exercise

For some people, the poem alone suffices. For others, the necessity of daily exercise, with failure ever ahead of them. Even if one falls back into the nightmare of empty days when one thinks only of oneself, attentive to pettiness, to one's own stomach, tiredness, boredom.

Beauty

Be it more or less bullied about, more or less exalted, flouted or not, within any kind of society and dependent on it, in revolt, ecstatic, on the margins, or awkwardly positioned, beauty will blossom everywhere.

Babbling

Unaware of the selective differentiations that language requires, an infant at first uses sounds as much for enchanting himself as for expressing himself (in response to outside solicitation). This primary function of the tongue (in the marvellous equivocation of the French word *langue*) is restored by poetry: whatever tragedy it is associated with, it withholds as much and even more by itself as by what it *means to say*.

Lucidity

Distrust (be it not disguised fear, moral rigidity, resentment, censor passing itself off as self-control) of intoxication (the plummeting should be different), of anthems, of anything—slogans, frenzied dancing, drunken binges of music or words—that galvanizes crowds.

It is merely a question of speaking clearly in the darkness. No language that is coded, initiatory, occult; no god or response emanating from murky depths. A return to Nerval not for the sentiment of some accursed power but, rather, for his willingness to bring to light (quite unsatisfactory terms) dream and insanity with the intention of dominating them.

Also distrust of those who are unaffected by the fear of the abyss, unless, like Ponge, they have been able to find a kind of health there, all the while acknowledging, without illusions, what is implied.

Ablutions

Ever cleansing ourselves of everything, getting lost, finding ourselves again amid a thousand fleeting impressions, *recreations*, various *micro-ecstasies* that fling us, for a split second, outside ourselves. Like ablutions made because we like water (its coolness, its caress) more than scrubbing ourselves clean.

Admirable, mentally, the cleanliness of children on whom neither prejudices, nor compartmentalizations, nor categories initially act. Doing one's best, as an adult, to get back to this state demands daily practice (the opposite of a habit).

To Exude

Mood, moroseness, futile preoccupations, anything keeping me remote from poetry—I attach myself to them, thinking I am ridding myself of them. Artificially exaggerated worries which are nothing in themselves and signs only of a lapse; a polluted poetic conscience, silently painful and apt to find excuses for itself.

Exoticness

Here, facing the blank page. Nowhere else. This waiting, this patient labour (futile exhaustion), this slightest spark. Nothing else. This in itself is radiance. The rest— upheavals, extraordinary events, outbursts of passion— originates in exoticness.

A feeling of poverty? Of being destitute yet eager to take sly revenge on those who will have lived more frenetically?

To be serenely the one to whom anything given can only be something lacking: as a result, to stop being miserable.

Blank Spaces

Someone having trouble seeing that the blank pages, inserted by the publisher between his poems in order to fill out a rather thin chapbook, *mean nothing, say nothing*, presupposes in turn, elsewhere, a specific meaning (but which one?) for blank spaces, and, for this very reason, fundamentally rejects them as such (what idea, therefore, of the poem?) as if reading, denying the gaps, could only be the impossible reconstitution of a willingly truncated text.

Blank spaces: often mere coquetry instead of a quest for or negation of meaning, whether (discreetly) canalized between lines of verse and strophes or (amounting to the same thing?) supremely pulverizing them: even then, it remains necessary to keep to the page, to a form through which our limits are staked out. (Otherwise, antics and impertinences.)

Inspiration

Letting the poem write itself.

Whatever form they take, constraints, inherent to poetry, are at no variance with it, disguising—indeed incompletely

—what is essential beneath—but what is to be said?—a groping search on the level of words.

From them, having everything to expect.

The feeling of being worked through (in the sense that one says *working through grief*) by an alien force as vital as the air with which, without thinking, we fill our lungs.

Inspiration? Unconscious? Terms, especially the latter, which are bedecked with theoretical references and denounce their own insufficiency.

Discontinuity

Discontinuity, yet taken up in a movement; a rupture and the effacement of the rupture; fragmentation—each part has its own life, from which wells up the appetite for wholeness; discourse which follows no straight line, but which, in one way or another, whenever buried, rises to the surface.

It is 'the indiligent reader', says Montaigne, who gets lost.

The One, the Multiple

The liking (appetite or nostalgia) for things in their variety or the aspiration that none of them stand out, that all of them merely imply.

The absolute (what lies behind this word?) or a pause in the need for the absolute. A contradiction in which we live, inside which, in the best moments, I manage not be bothered any more as if, effacing itself, it temporarily no longer had any hold.

Opening from the Inside

Several things all at once, vaguely. There is no question of giving in to verbal imaginativeness (yet in fact there is, from another angle) but, rather, of entering, polarized, the world of words because of an outside shock, which can also make one founder. A little like wanting to get inside a house whose doors and windows are shut. The key is missing, the image or the sentence that would give flight, even if this means not taking one's place at the beginning, indeed ultimately of being eliminated.

Future (yet having already taken place as well, for whoever reads it), the poem is closed, not cramped. Once inside the house, one opens it up completely. Light and air circulate just as soon.

String Quartet

Instruments so closely related that they are differentiated incompletely or, rather, grasped through their resemblances. Adding an instrument of another kind breaks the equilibrium.

[Bartók: the discordant sounds, the tension are such that in places anyone devoting his absolute attention to the whole piece would collapse, wrenched apart.]

Thickness of Meaning

The primary meaning is little needed by a metaphor, a figure of speech, an idiotism, which, however, retain us only if we sense in them the thickness of a meaning. From that very life, dreams, poems and works of art unfurl in us.

Sieves

To the point where no coherence justifies images, themes, syntax, etc.

Yet no poem, no work of art, no human undertaking offers anything, seemingly, that is totally inexplicable, irreducible to some decoding key (or several, when a single one is insufficient).

Only what does not remain at the bottom of our sieves possesses life, genuinely possesses—intuitive—meaning. A reason to put them aside? On the contrary. The finer the sieve is, the more precious what it lets sift through.

Parentheses

Partitions that open a gap without separating, minor obstacles, breeding grounds, inside pockets of the sentence which, despite these hindrances, moves forward, flows like water, backing up here, rushing into a gully there. From inside to outside, minute or excessive, the distance varies constantly, ever needing to be re-evaluated.

The entrance can be missed—the crossing, the leap—out of faulty approximation. The reading is, or almost, rereading, requiring that one start all over again.

Inside these thin, always double, sometimes barely perceptible, sometimes almost impassable partitions, sensibility needs to be exerted as a way of passing through, of gliding along, which gives one the feeling of being retained, although temporarily, and, just as much, of being led.

Italics (to my mind) disturb the harmony and unity of the text. The same goes for dashes, which stand out too overtly, isolating, putting aside, acknowledging that one is leaping from one thing to another. A single dash can suffice; the feeling of disarticulation increases accordingly.

Promising the opposite, parentheses plane down, level out, just show on the surface even if there is a leap, saying something radically different only by inserting it into the flow of language. Parentheses form an incision in the flesh of the sentence, an indentation, a crack through which rises an inner voice (italics, if need be, in this case), a voice that is foreign yet exerts no authority, is almost clandestine and in any event muffled, allusive, murmuring. Parentheses possess no status of their own, can only come in between, intervening in no cowardly way but, rather, (if this can be said without pejorative connotations), from *below*, ready to beat a retreat, to go back into their shell.

Parentheses imply their self-effacement at the very instant that they appear, bearing their own end in themselves; are ephemeral, knowing and avowing that they are so, expressing things from elsewhere yet within a familiar remark.

Speaking is thus called into question from within by another, *subconscious*, kind of speaking whose discretion recalls that of the slightest signs, most of them going unnoticed, emanating from our nights, from our dreams, from who knows where, as fleeting as they are unexpected. Stubborn, perhaps, the signs never press the point too much, like brief sounds of a doorbell ever ringing through the tissue of our consciousness whenever we refuse to pay attention to them, ever (by definition) in the wrong. Parentheses offer a similar snag.

The discontinuity principle of parentheses is also different from that of ellipses. The sentence neither dies out nor fades away among the sands. It is not sectioned, yet, as we know beforehand, it must once again get the upper hand. The surface turmoil is less (yet what is hiding in the depths?). Similarly, our state of consciousness (consisting, however, of nothing else) is hardly disturbed, seemingly, by the minor accidents of which I am speaking.

Let's take leaps, fragmentation and interruptions as essential elements for poetry, as well as the approach to the oneiric sources on which they might well depend, like a desire to follow in its apparent chaos the surging forth (I cannot say the flow) of thought (thought is not the right word). Outside and inside with their imprecise margins, with their fluctuating impermeableness, move away from each other or come back together until they merge. It's not that parentheses in themselves carry the poetry, never ascribable to anything; at best parentheses will be good guides, especially where paths of prose are taken.

Spiritual Progress

Surpass—absolute incentive—what is personal in the emotion; the poem should surmount the emotion, lead it beyond itself until its own origin is forgotten.

The Right Space

Seek in everything the right distance, an accord, free, breathable space. Float, be *suspended* like a body in liquid, thoughtless—the state of alertness to the poem.

Equality

Between the elements put to work, between the two terms of an image, whether the accent is placed on their identity or on their 'differential qualities', between the subject and the object, even between the word and the thing or between he who writes and he who reads, poetry presupposes a relationship between equals, or an ever-present reciprocity.

Love also presupposes that it is at the right level, although dominator and dominated, torturer and victim, can join together as they please (I do not say freely).

Nothing secondary, subordinate, auxiliary down to the slightest article, the slightest pronoun. Am I wrong to see this as the very heart of the poetic, or amorous, experience, upon which one can attempt to found any other kind of relationship? Unless this is thus a mere projection of an inability to feel, and consciously put, myself in a situation which consists as much of superiority as inferiority and to which everything, in every moment, tends to return. Yet (Lao Tzu): 'The weak overcomes the strong.'

On the Spot

Out of the water, in a flash, the countless, unpredictable leaps of spawning fish defy all order, yet are dictated by a necessity. Whoever observes them is constantly deceived and yet, if inattentive, would overlook them.

Such is also poetic consciousness, both anterior and future: what it watches out for has already happened, takes on value only after the event.

Inner Voice

Poetry is the voice of the *I*, an inner voice, without an interlocutor; the other person, who receives it, hears it as his own voice, as his own neither narrative, nor discursive, nor theatrical words.

Things, in Their Variety

The infinite variety of beings and things in their singularity, their contingency: a willow, the elm seen from the window, a thousand nothings (this is not the word) on which to whet our attention: this wall here, this pile of rocks for their own sake, without regard for the *notions* of wall, rock—on the contrary, shoving them around, pulling them down to position them once again, the need to understand necessarily sooner or later, alas, getting the upper hand once again.

Things, in Their Obviousness

A waterfall which, interminably, musters its sparkles, its noise twisting around itself with its hollows, its slight bulges, indeed, provided that the words strike home, re-creating upon each reading their object, that hearth we possess of images, impressions, shifting associations.

So that the waterfall, a mere pretext, does not represent the words turned back on themselves, the poem having become its own story, etc. Too obvious ruts, truths to be inferred at best, springboards for going beyond.

[But from there to the flimsiness of some poems which, with their gnawed wings, seemingly wish to restrict themselves to banal reporting . . .]

Sterility

Because it alone has to express everything, every poem misses its target, transferring this hope to another poem, already leading to the threshold of the same failure, indefinitely reducing any attempt (of what else would we be capable?) to mere wasted words, scraps, peelings.

Writing, reading: ever beginning again—and ever differently—out of fear of grasping nothing? Out of dread, fear of the void, increasing the number of barriers.

Only the gap between each poem, between each word, can save, like a fatality (futile remedy), and as a result (but the bet is never won) it is a wager of renewal.

Things, in Their Incoherence

How to preserve in words the (at least apparent) incoherence of things that are simply there, in their disorder, unconcerned about what they might mean, in a poem in which they are empowered to be present? Needed here is the sentiment that they belong to an ensemble, without which they will fall to ashes, and the poem with them. Everything here must (despite appearances) hold together thanks to what the inner radiance of a meaning will allow.

Let things *speak*: a futile desire, going against their nature and that of poetry. Futile as well the self-reproach that I utter about always seeking to come full circle.

Unique

At this moment, the mountain, this mountain looming in front of me and, inversely, this void (all? nothing?) which gives to the mountain its value and to which I reach out entirely, this other thing (inappropriate terms) that is still the mountain and, at the same time, negates it, is simply *nothing else* . . .

The Same and the Other

The body, the pleasure of the Other in order to— unbelievable gratitude!—give my own body back to me, my own pleasure. Inside, outside, identity, otherness, cease being distinct. The hand, wholly itself, becomes hip (impalpable limit!), shoulder, back.

Geode

Its outside retains no one's attention. Fascinating beauty of the jagged edges that are revealed only through an irreparable fracture, or effraction.

Orpheus

Entrenching oneself, excluding oneself (voluntary temporary exile, yet which, without one's being able to find encouragement from it, right away, must also be a path leading to others); going down into the depths of oneself like a dreamer into the depths of his dream, yet (major difference) without abandoning an extreme vigilance.

The poem is the reinvented dream, the mirror of the dream.

Desert

Poetry as 'a flamboyant form of life' (Reverdy). Or dejection? Inner rotting? Retreat into the desert, refuge remote from everyone, in addition in a language more or less aloof from the spoken language. A dive into the mirror from which no image emerges. Above all, more solemnly (should one see this as poetic justice?), growing indifference towards to the world, its affairs, its agitation, sterile or not.

Even at that, if the *ego* had been given notice . . .

Blank Spaces

Going down all the way to where there is nothing more to say, the origin and incentive that the poem is before words, that founds it, roots it (taking away all roots), throws it into language by means of an indraught.

Psychological Desert

Swimmer unconcerned about—not unaware of—the depth. Like haiku, rich with what it doesn't say, doesn't have to say, and has made futile in order to pay attention only to the plunk of a frog diving into water.

Two Parts

On second thought, the part of shadow; for the poem, phrased otherwise, the happy part, even (at best?) remaining *in the air*, inhaled, unwritten.

Daily Gestures

Thinking of death. But of what? Naming the unnamable? Giving—or lending—existence, by means of a word, to nothingness? Absence, however, in which we stand firm, against which we are never finished reassuring ourselves even in trifles, slightest habits, gestures and familiar objects that conceal the unknown and make us believe in our perpetuity (an illusion about which a part of us doesn't manage to be fooled).

Something else again is the flash of lightning that *projects us beyond* into pleasure, emotion, orgasm, ecstasy (more words). That feeling, then, of really living. No more need for pathetic crutches. Intensity and detachment might then indeed merge.

Diversity

Behind the screen of things and beings—their multiplicity, their variety—reigns the same undifferentiated void.

How would the unbelievable diversity of food correspond to fasting? Or to silence, words, speech, intonations, languages, noises, sounds? Incomprehensible diversity; incomprehensible fractioning, incomprehensible abyss of a being or a thing, from one moment to the next.

This is precisely what reassures because of its factual nature, and disturbs once it is faced with its opposite.

Nymphs

Sylphids, *nymphs*, *naiads*, figures (already such, perhaps, to the eyes of the Ancients) thanks to whom external reality (just convenient terms) is animated in its diversity, its singularity. Not abstractly: such and such a stream, woods, not all places, but those to which is attached (illusorily or not, what does it matter?) a spirit.

Exercises

Études and *variations* conducive to moving one deeply— miracle!—even conceived as pure exercises (which is not always the case). Enough to make one think about the emotion (called aesthetic, for want of anything better) born of music itself.

Ambiguity

In a world ruled by the necessity of settling matters with a *yes* or a *no*, a poem—a prosecution witness for all the simplistic forces—says nothing except in ambiguous terms.

Eddies

The water near the shore gathers and breaks apart into various smaller eddies, renewed, uncompleted. In order to express them, such is the sentence, the poem (awaited, forthcoming) with its suspense, its parentheses, its second thoughts. May beneath these opposing movements that harm each other, that destroy each other on the surface, reign a mass sweeping them along, bringing them into being, ensuring all continuity.

Baroque Style

May words, sentences, sounds, movements, ruptures, appeals, oppositions, whirlpools, should they fail to be the respiration, the life of the water itself, find a way to be— indeed, by mimesis—the verbal equivalent.

Basting Thread

Already things were taking shape. Everything fades away, vanishes. The feeling persists of having been inattentive.

Also of having been swindled in a cowardly way, though it is not clear how, of one's own life.

The Proof Is in the Void

Poetry enables no contact with the things it names, but only with the words. (Du Bellay's *Les Regrets* is already exemplary, though perhaps not without a point of affectation here and there.) Poetry arouses a desire which it cannot fulfil, of which even the meaning is lacking.

Narcissism

A poetry that silences the *ego*, that gives the ego its notice without oppressing it. Subjective consciousness is not at stake (experiencing oneself as being alive in and through what, as an *object*, is *obstructive*) but, rather, egoistical withdrawal into oneself.

Language has its traps: writing that bites its own tail; other forms of narcissism.

Reader

From an anonymous reader, absent, out of sight, don't we expect more than from just anyone? Don't we demand total adherence, like that of an *alter ego*? And don't we come to writing because we have been disappointed, egoistically, by others?

Writing genuinely can only be beyond, when the reader, totally freed, has stopped mattering (except to himself).

Oblivion, Obliteration

Oblivion: the disappearance of the memory by erosion, or by alluvial deposits; in the latter, adding (even piling up, obstructing) instead of taking away. Obliterate has both meanings, which amount to the same: texts would be erased by scratching the parchment, so that it could be written on again.

Facteur Cheval

Is it the finished work that counts, or the forty years of efforts come hell or high tide against everything and everyone? Is it the awkwardness or the overall success? The naivety or the genius (a perhaps unfounded opposition)? The excessiveness, the daydreamer's insanity regarding those in his midst? Who else was this creative artist for those close to him but a crank, probably a bore, a disgrace and the laughing stock of the county? Without ceasing to admire to him, would one wish to have been Cheval?

Verse

A poem, that miracle of equilibrium as fragile as a card castle, as strong as a tubular construction; no more made of incoherent words jotted down on paper than forming a sequence from which nothing should escape comprehension; in which the lines of verse suffice unto themselves and, whatever the gap between them, are inscribed in a whole; in which, however discreet they may be, echoes create an inner distance (how to define it?)

Transfers—like metaphors—and comparisons, identity or similitude, harmony, contrasts.

Effacement

To disappear: wishing not so much to efface one's own tracks as to stake out the place where one disappears, to command attention negatively. The opposite of keeping out of the limelight.

Body and Soul

'I see your prick, my love.' Probably nothing else in this hastily scribbled graffiti (*see*, or *suck*?) than a schoolchild's prank, yet it is a well-turned phrase. Asserting itself unaffectedly is a demand for pleasure which deservingly takes the male for a target and, in contrast to so many ordinary, vulgar or servile phrases, finds intensity and strength of conviction in the simple present tense. A serene, straightforward assertion demolishing the distinction between *low* and *high*. Everything, all at once, in broad daylight, and may the devil take any interjection—*O* or *Oh my love*! A caesura, a phrasing, eloquently balances and alone links the two sides of the six-syllable line like two parts of a human being, body and soul (also eloquent, the precedence that language grants to the first term over the second one) or, to detour to a reputedly sensual kind of music (thanks to a famous theme), *body and soul*.

Soap Bubbles

Ever more transparent before bursting by dint of thinness. Elimination of the *ego* through limpidity, the absence of thickness. Not wishing to grasp: the opposite of barricading oneself.

Blank Page

Waiting until a sort of vibration, or trembling, occurs— produced from where? From within me? From outdoors? Talismanic illusion? It doesn't matter. Space itself becomes something else, at once full and empty. Impression of dreaming and wakefulness, of neither dreaming nor wakefulness.

Dark Clarity

Ultimately shadow, far from contradicting light, ensures its passage. Likewise, eddies lead the current on or, in a sentence, parentheses not so much fetters as guarantees of fluidity.

A poem lives from what—below or beyond words—burns it, *blows it out*, gives birth to it, chaos having been overcome.

Chance

To owe everything to a stroke of chance; to give oneself over to chance, not without having attempted the impossible in order to overcome it. To rummage through the night, aided only by the dark lantern of words and with no ambition other than that of creating a river ford.

Belonging to the World

This vibration—trembling and joy, anguish, flux, upheaval—is the awareness of a blow, tottering, toppling backwards on itself, facing its negation.

Empty

'There is the question and, at the end, the despair of a rejected response.' (Jabès) Without evading it, without losing anything of an ever-active attentiveness and seriousness, to work even in the slightest circumstances at freeing oneself from such a helpless feeling.

The Call of the Wild

Determined to demolish, destroy, to disown our past (and by this, acknowledging it), deprived of a ruler, of a rule (while, on another level, the latest trend is one of the most restrictive ones), haunted by anti-art (negatively, by art), by deconstruction (which runs counter to construction), have we perhaps returned to a sort of state of nature, to the ABCs, as shown by other signs as well? At the heart of such disorder (should we investigate it?), 'what does beauty represent'? No response brings this question to a close, seals the gap. At best, a locus of uncertainty might be designated. We nonetheless have to reinvent our origins. We can believe in our pseudo-savagery merely as a myth where our excess of civilization or at best the hope of a renewal can be read in reverse.

Much more confounding, amid over inflated values, is how the most extreme rigor serves the most poignant delirium in Alban Berg's *Wozzeck*; or this by Mandelstam in regard to one of the subtlest *oeuvres* of all times: 'If the halls of the Hermitage suddenly went mad, if the paintings of all the schools, of all the masters, abruptly taken down from their nails, should intermingle and fuse, filling the air of the rooms with a futurist howl, with violently agitating colours, we would obtain something similar to *The Divine Comedy.*'

Caesura

Extraordinary impression of an abyss, of having just been aroused from a very short nap. With no delay, with no transition between two contiguous moments, the water-tightness is total, the interruption, brutal.

On the contrary, sometimes the passage is almost imperceptible, the first moment extending into the second one, yet denatured, diverted most unexpectedly, although coherent at the time.

In the same state, different.

Writing

The opposite of a simple, self-evident movement, writing always stakes out a distance while wanting to efface it. It is not the act marred by inauthenticity that I too often believe it to be but, rather, being born of something torn apart, it is the very act of a consciousness inclined to founder, to burn what separates it from its object.

In this sense, social maladjustment (*write and hide away* in Jean-Jacques Rousseau's terms), doesn't account for every poetic vocation.

Negation

No negation (*nothing*, *no*, *not any*, etc.) that does not pass through affirmation; likewise, absence is a presence which is rejected, gnawed away, hollow, which a void inhabits—animates?—defines.

Likewise, a poem.

Reiterating

Reiteration, a remedy for precariousness: a kind of permanence (no matter the illusion) is created.

Paradise

This extreme peace, suspense, porosity, transparency— and the fear of missing it; screen, abyss, a sinking into the obscurity.

Lacking a Baroque Style

Not *rendering* through words the movement, the sparkle, the noise of water, not wanting to mime—physically, as it were—the eddies, the fits and starts, but never ceasing to reach out to them out of concern for the sentence, the poem, their—should one say prosodic?—demands, as opposed to a baroque style (if it may be defined by the priority given to form). Not acting as if things could be present in words or as if their presence could spring from a simulation.

Beyond the field subjected to our control, after concluding work that aims for the most rigorously apt inspiration, thanks to the relative discretion of words, alert not to divert towards themselves the attention to which their object is entitled, perhaps water will find itself, by chance, to be tender, bubbling, lithe, massive, aspiring, lazy.

Being faithful to language, to its laws, its limits, in order to be brought back to things more securely? The opposite of what could be equated to cantilevers, *trompe-l'oeil* and other devices obviously counting on illusion to make something *seem real*.

Round Trip

To write down what you experience or in order to attain what you experience, to respond to it. No less, to experience what is written, to find truth there, unexpectedly.

Reflection

Metaphysical reflection (this is not what makes *Les Chimères* miraculous) without contradicting poetry will always remain outside it; outside that abandon, that sensibility, that part taken from words and from the singular experience provoking them as well as that struggle.

Inflammation

To the extent that thinking is pursued, I cannot view it as anything but a sort of inflammation: one idea leads to another, ideas follow upon each other, piling up, from which excitement results more or less, an itching sensation, turgidity.

Poetic Consciousness

Grace taking effect upon awakening (but was no preparation necessary?), like a sky whose clouds have been removed during the night, now completely clear.

Doesn't such grace merge with the sentiment that everything is connected and belongs to me—or that I belong to everything? The desire to be everywhere at once, but (instead of wishing to dash here and there) awareness of plenitude experienced where I am (wherever it is) in this very moment (whichever it is, one can say).

Already, in fact, a secret pain burns in me, of having to lose what I am given (that's something done), of having, in order to re-establish communication, to launch the ark of a poem.

Sullen skies, perhaps, in less than an hour.

Narrow Path

If possible, a poem just like a mountain path at once safe, narrow, steep, sometimes barely staked out. Landmarks are rare. Imperiously, in the difficult passages, any mis-step is excluded; the hike requires all one's attention (day-dreamer, no absent-minded reading!), yet in some places the walking becomes easier without resting or a moment of abandon signifying relinquishment.

Tension, slowness, time unwinding without impatience, and if the places where one treads become narrower (nothing in excess from one word to the next), what spaces the eyes engrave themselves into, spaces ever vaster as one climbs and always different!

Ys

When the poem is engulfed, the page recovers its blank-ness. Speaking without saying any more.

Was a wound; a momentum.

Clearing Everything Away

Outside of books. Outside of books only, even if writing necessarily leads back to them, but in order to give our-selves over to the outdoors just as soon.

Poetry: synonym of clearing everything away.

Effusion

Enchantment, exhilaration, the delicious feeling of touching a promised land, of merely having to let oneself be borne along. Time no longer exists; the hand is no longer separated from the page on which the poem is being written. Impossible, however, as obstacles and torment soon re-emerge, to get back—pure effusion, pure outflow—to the initial momentum. One needs to domesticate, stop, pin down, get down to work, which is no longer a process of becoming but (in only one sense) an outcome, no longer vertigo but a buried fervour, an adjustment, where concern about being followed comes into play.

How to be genuine?

Outdoors

The pleas of one of my primary-school teachers not to spend our days confined at home sometimes come back to me. Should I chuckle about them? Whatever (at times despairing) hours of self-confinement ensue, the fact remains that poetry takes shape outdoors, it requires hitting the road, heading across fields.

The same exercise, yet inverted, is that of the Buddhist monk who applies himself to remain undistracted by his thought (or absence of thought), by a birdsong, the flight of an insect, the play of light and shadow in the foliage of a tree.

Titles

To give—or not to give—a title to a poem: a mysterious, delicate, never resolved operation of deliberate intentions.

Arriving afterwards, the title by no means sums up the poem to which it is linked by secret affinities, no more (on the contrary) than it limits its extensions or stretches its meaning. However, the title encloses the poem even as a frame confines a painting, sealing it off, isolating it, a stone associated by the current to other stones filling the streambed.

Otherwise (as indeed can happen) the pieces of the same book overlap.

Vital

What is a poem worth in regard to the total disappearance (thus less unimaginable, more tangible, than if I speak of *death*) to which each of us is destined? This is the only scale of measurement: Which words must not be sacrificed for anything in the world?

More generally (but this is to speak rashly), what credence should be given to something that would lose all its force in these times of failure, suffering, hardship? It would then be too late to resuscitate poetic consciousness itself, a flame that is insufficiently kept burning from day to day and is necessary, vital.

Until then may one be filled with joy (ever the lesson of haiku) by the attention paid to a bright ember after rainfall or to the plunk of a frog diving into water.

French Clarity

'What is conceived well is expressed clearly.' A proposition to be read the other way around: the clarity of the wording gives thought its own clarity while whittling it back.

Discontinuity

Ellipses interrupt too half-heartedly a text that is getting bogged down; whereas blank spaces which are franker, clear-cut without always uncovering the edge of a rupture, beckon to be used like a ford. In the final reckoning, dashes, which are abrupt, would suit me better.

Moreover, by dint of such cuts, hasn't one encroached on the reader who is, otherwise, freer to speed up or slow down the pace, to open all windows, as he pleases, onto his reverie?

Unexplainable

'Because he was he and I was I.' But the points where differences occur also plunge into obscurity.

I

Wouldn't relinquishing the first-person singular in order to prevent the subject from settling in at the heart of the poem to the detriment of the object with which he intends to blend; that is, expressly relinquishing the first-person singular—as this need has come to me—actually consecrate, instead of working towards the effacement of the subject, its sovereignty since the *you* would be eliminated in the same stroke?

I thought I had especially viewed the *I* as an intermediary, indeed a hyphen between the reader's consciousness and what it heads for, but also as an obstacle to being immediately addressed, as it happens in Caspar David Friedrich's paintings where the spectator is repositioned in the foreground by his double, seen from behind like the 'Monk by the Sea' who is gazing, in his place, at the haze and blurry waves.

Inebriation

Avidly drinking with one's eyes (as the saying goes) the light and all that it bathes with its unity, the stream flooding among the trees and at once shiny and dull, the houses, the neighbouring hillsides, all things at the heart of the present.

Including even the transparency of the air and its coolness —the effervescence, in passing, on the surface of being!—this moment unfurls like a gulp of an intense, heady, sparkling white wine: well-being, excitement and inner reverberation all soon destroyed by the need, the vain desire, to prolong them.

A moment of drunkenness, indeed, a slight inebriation (is there anything more delicious?) superior to that which wine can set one (yet poetry also has its non-drinkers) because the senses are more surely sharpened and will not become dull after having been titillated.

Coming Up As Close As Possible

In the depths of oneself (no contradiction about that), coming as close as possible to what is real, at the heart of words, seeking their point of convergence. Not the *real* (if one means making no gesture to philosophy), but reality wrongly called 'outer'; not exactly the *heart* of words, but the obscure origin from which, at best, they can be drawn up to the surface.

Rough Drafts

Marvellously, afterwards, to retrieve the intonations of a lost voice, to follow once again the tracks of how it all came to light—uncertainties, tumults, trial and error yet with the self-assurance this time that it will all be sorted out. What was laboriously lugged from dark swamps will surely blossom in the sunlight of inspiration.

How can these pages be destroyed?

Yet this share of what has been gone through and expended to nourish the poem is now mere detritus (what's the use of relics?), exuding only death, decomposition, nothingness.

The work will catch fire again in other ways, unfurl, come back to life from word to word for its reader—in him, through him—who alone will free it from the fate of being set aside, of remaining fixed, immobile in a *Sleepy Hollow*—a guarantee of renewal against the overflow and despairs that produced the work.

Speaking

It speaks for itself! A gesture, a landscape, a photograph, a revealing blunder, a style of dressing, etc.—the expression always designates that which escapes words, takes place or expresses itself apart from them. Moving water, passing clouds, a piece of music, a face all *speak for themselves* without us having to wonder how they occur or what they are saying to the world. In the same straight-away manner—poems. Éluard, 'One dreams about a poem as one dreams about a human being.'

The Last Word

Both running to the very end and wishing to postpone the deadline. Except when reading, among other activities, is a mere means of obtaining information, its goal—or its goal in only an ambiguous sense—is not this equally feared and expected final notice (less so in poetry, where the mind is rarely held on a leash), this death, *the last word* that every sentence, every breath, nears and should rescue: a double necessity, a double desire standing up against itself, and for that very reason guaranteeing intensity.

Not only where there are overt blanks or ruptures, but also in prose where the discourse seems to unfold continuously, it is jolts, slowdowns, leaps forward, second guesses, halts and suspended moments that constitute the very pace of the text, at the very least of how it is read.

Space and Movement

The bustling of seagulls around the jetty, chasing each other without respite, squabbling while suddenly swerving, dodging, attacking, screeching above a lake whipped by the wind . . . Even the opposite shore, blending with the long strides of the clouds, no longer seems to stay still. One cannot help but be swept into the movement.

'Elasticity of space' (as has been written apropos of Claude Lorrain); its quietude or, just as well, its absence of calm.

Liquidness

Language has a water-like elasticity, fluidity, force and passiveness, ethereal lightness (its transparency) and heaviness when it falls massively, ready for anything.

Disorderly, coming to light after uncontrollable underground passages, it nonetheless continues to have a share in the sky. The very image of the continuity of life— wellspring and depletion—ever in motion, in danger of spilling over, of going astray, smitten by whatever resists, it spurts upward only in order to spread out even better. What is marked on its surface is effaced, renewed, repeated, varying ad infinitum. It has always said everything and has everything to say with mildness or violence, abandon or authority (yet an authority that is never acquired, never established). Despite its transparency, it does not reveal its depth, or only deceivingly so; and when everything can be read clearly, it is the distance between language and things that defies accurate assessment.

Isn't it our ambition, immoderately, to build works as lasting as stone monuments from what flows between our fingers—which we never will truly be able to appropriate, which, at best, lends itself to us, to our desires, our whims, our games—from what does not *hold* together?

Becoming

The *oeuvre* must be built according to a coherent plan that is reliable or unreliable, at first inexistent and long, or all the way to the end, obscure. Ever ahead of us, subsequently, as ahead of the reader, it can only be a quest, a becoming.

Truism. The same goes for the meaning of life and human relations; thus for all things.

Depth

To deepen, to entertain with others—human beings and things—*deep* relationships, to descend rather *deeply* into oneself: to head for what is essential.

Indeed, but sliding across the surface out of fear of *sinking*, growing heavier, getting bogged down? Out of fear of offering, of meeting up, only slight resistance?

Such is the flight of the bird dominating—without ignoring—the abyss.

Ardour

Having come that far—as much when reading as when writing, up to that point, that genuine outcome where one feels oneself at the heart of a conflagration. Imperiously. The rest, which is only ashes or half-burnt shavings, cannot retain.

Negative Inspiration

To aspire to: to reach out to an object. Even if the fervour, the attentiveness, indeed the submissiveness and (much more than the pride) the humility at stake are equivalent in value, *aspiration* (without unduly exaggerating the words) can lack a response, as opposed to *inspiration* through which the divine spirit is received. One is the drawback of the other: negative inspiration.

Outdoor Table

As if under the shelter of trees, beech and pine, from which the view embraces the whole area, on this makeshift table made of salvaged boards, in a place long held in affection and balancing light and shadow, as if on this outdoor table for the use of whoever might have the whim to interrupt his walk and, on the spot, fasten down a flight of words—or at noon, some day labourer, hired on by the nearby vineyard, coming to sit down, alone or not, although a bench has been provided on only one side—as if the notebook that almost replaces a companion for me, a talisman perhaps, had been forgotten there, a plaything of the wind which, without being able to close the notebook again, kept, keeps, leafing through it.

Full Margins

p. 13. Chappuis refers to the general atmosphere of the poems written by French poet Pierre Reverdy (1889–1960), not necessarily to the well-known line from the poem 'Pendule', *Sable mouvant* (1959): 'Dans l'air chaud du plafond, la rampe des rêves s'allume' (In the warm air of the ceiling, the ramp of dreams lights up).

p. 53. Paul Klee (1879–1940) was a German artist whose style was influenced by Surrealism, Cubism and Expressionism.

Blind Distance

A first version of this book was published by Éditions Robert in 1974. This translation has been made from the José Corti edition (2000).

The sequence ends with this dedication:

> dedicated in 1974
> > to René Char ('Like the Summer')
> > to Dominique Lévy & André Siron
> > > ('Garden of Delights')
> > to Rachel & Jean-Pierre Jelmini
> > > ('The Emptiness of Words')
> > to Jean-Pierre Burgart ('The Harrow of
> > > Looking')

to Ernest Geller ('Another Lark')
to Philippe Jaccottet ('August Orchard')

Today [2000]
to Florian Rodari ('Clearing')
to Michel Collot ('Neighboring nor
Faraway')
to Claude Dourguin ('Placeless,
Dateless')

'May phrases taken by chance and as if anonymously from Martin Heidegger, Giuseppe Ungaretti, Paul Éluard, Maurice Blanchot, and Jean Laude be recognized and paid tribute to in the margins.'

p. 96. *The Balance of the Daylight.* '... *the noise of cars driving through the cluse*'. 'Cluse' is the geological term for a gorge cut perpendicularly or transversely through an otherwise continuous mountain ridge.

Abstracted from Time

A first version of this book was published by Éditions Empreintes in 1990. This translation has been made from the Empreintes paperback edition (2005).

At the beginning of the sequence, Chappuis adds the dedication:

To Albert-E. Yersin
(*as if he were still among us*)
for the drawings that inspired
the first texts in this series

To Anne and Gérard Macé
for 'the ambivalence of dreams and words'

To Florian Rodari
for a chance encounter recalled here

To the memory of my mother
for the 'Solitary Stroller's' shadow
blended with her thoughts

The epigraph by the German poet Novalis (1772–1801) is found in *Aphorismen und Fragmente* (1798–1800).

p. 149. *Memory, Scattered Mirror*. In this text, Chappuis recalls the song 'Allons danser sous les ormeaux' (Let's dance beneath elms), from Jean-Jacques Rousseau's one-act opera *Le Devin du village* (1752), which his mother used to sing.

p. 154. *A Remote Greeting*. The poem alludes to the poet's feelings during a concert (which included one of Schubert's quartets) when, at the same moment, he learnt of his friend's death.

The Black of Summer

p. 186. *Noon Fanfares*. The epigraph by the French poet Paul Éluard (1895–1952) is the title of his book *Sommes-nous deux ou suis-je solitaire* (1959), with etchings by the Swiss artist Hans Erni. The term 'ritornello' has several meanings in music; here it signifies a refrain or an interlude.

p. 188. *Fatality of Water*. Chappuis alludes to Robert Schumann's suicide attempt on 27 February 1854 by jumping into the Rhine near Düsseldorf. The *Märchenbilder* (or *Fairy Tale Pictures*) is Schumann's 1851 composition for piano and viola (opus 113).

p. 190. *April*. The German expression *Schade* means 'what a pity', 'what a shame'. 'Schade, ich verstehe nicht' means 'what a shame. I don't understand'.

The sequence ends with this dedication:

> *Once Again*, *Absent* to Anne Perrier & Jean Hutter, in which they will find the memory of a painting by Pierre Bonnard.

> *Voices and Cowbells* to Bertrand & Fabienne Fillaudeau.

> *On Charles Bridge* to Jean-Édouard Augsburger, Petr Herel & Dagmar Halasova, who entered into a dialogue about this short text, in Losne, at Thierry Bouchard's atelier in 1997.

> *April* to Philippe Jaccottet, first in *Écriture 40* as an echo to the 'child colours lavishly handed out, morning colours' which unfurl in 'Apparition of Flowers' (*Notebook of Greenery*).

> *Tangible reality* to Pierre Romnée in order to contemplate with him, with the same gaze, the *Landscape with Three Trees*, an engraving by Rembrandt.

Within the Voice's Reach

p. 212. The title *Fermata*—'point d'orgue' in the original—refers to the symbol of 'hold' or 'pause' in musical notations.

Cuts

Some pieces in this volume previously appeared in a chapbook titled *Le ciel sans cicatrices* (2013). This translation has been made from the José Corti edition (2014).

The French title *Entailles* offers a fine example of the semantic resonance that is difficult to render with a single English word. *Entailles* suggests 'nicks', 'notches', 'gashes', 'incisions' and 'cuts'. I have chosen the latter because of Chappuis's frequent allusion to something indicating a break, a rupture, a line or a barrier. The other potential solutions are too specific.

p. 253. *Blurred Landscape* is closely linked to Jean-Baptiste-Camille Corot's *cliché-verre*, *Souvenir d'Ostie* (1855), which belongs to the collection of the Cabinet des estampes, Musée d'art et d'histoire (Museum of Art and History) in Geneva.

p. 257. Reverdy's phrase '*the unscarred sky*', quoted as an epigraph, and the line 'everything tears apart', belong to the poem 'Le circuit de la route' (from *Coeur de chêne*, 1921).

p. 280. Fukuda Chiyo-ni (1703–75), the famous Japanese haiku poet from the Edo period (1603–1867). Her works exemplify the notion of 'oneness with nature'.

p. 313. *The Slightest Unevenness of the Ground* alludes to a locality called Les Coeuries in the mountains near Neuchâtel, Switzerland.

The Proof Is in the Void

p. 320. *The Contents of Words.* Marcel Proust (1871–1922) invents the verbal expressions 'faire catleya' and 'arranger les catleyas', which both mean 'to make love', in the second section (Un amour de Swann) of *Du côté de chez Swann* (1913). The 'cattelya' (Proust writes the word with one 't') is the genus of over a hundred species of orchids mostly found in the Caribbean and South America.

p. 322. *Covering Over the Tracks.* Edmond-Henri Crisinel (1897–1948) was an important Swiss poet and writer.

p. 325. *Babbling.* The French word *langue* means both 'tongue' and 'language'.

p. 325. *Lucidity.* Chappuis refers to the writers Gérard de Nerval (1808–55) and Francis Ponge (1899–1988).

p. 328. *Discontinuity*. The phrase 'indiligent reader' is mentioned in Montaigne's essay 'On Vanity' (1580).

p. 329. *String Quartet*. The Hungarian maestro Béla Bartók (1881–1945) composed six string quartets.

p. 333. *Equality*. 'The weak overcomes the strong' is one of the best-known paradoxes formulated by Lao Tzu (or Laozi), the sixth-century Chinese philosopher who wrote the *Tao Te Ching*.

p. 338. *Desert*. 'a flamboyant form of life'. In his 'Lettre-préface pour *L'Oeuvre poétique de Pierre Reverdy* par Emma Stojkovic' (1951), Reverdy writes: 'La poésie est une forme flamboyante de la vie'. The text is included in the volume *Cette emotion appelée poésie* (1974).

p. 342. *The Proof Is in the Void*. Joachim du Bellay (1522–60) wrote *Les Regrets* during a sojourn in Rome in 1553–57 and published it upon his return to France in 1558.

p. 342. *Narcissism*. The phrase 'writing that bites its own tail' refers to the ancient symbol of ouroboros, which depicts a snake or a dragon biting its own tail. It often represents self-reflexivity and circularity in the sense of re-creation or the phenomena of regeneration in nature.

p. 343. *Facteur cheval*. The title refers to Ferdinand Cheval (1836–1924), the postman ('facteur' means postman) who spent thirty-three years of his life building his 'Ideal Palace' in Hauterives, France; and subsequently eight years constructing his tomb. Both are considered masterpieces of naïve architecture.

p. 346. *Empty*. 'There is the question and, at the end, the despair of a rejected response'. The entire *oeuvre* of the French poet Edmond Jabès (1912–91), and notably his *Book of Questions* (1963–73), revolves around 'questions' and the impossibility of receiving a 'response'.

p. 347. *The Call of the Wild.* The opera *Wozzeck* (1925) by Alban Berg (1885–1935) is known for its avant-garde style of presenting violence, brutality and sadism on stage. Osip Mandelstam (1891–1938), the Russian poet, wrote these lines in *Conversation on Dante* (1967; written in 1933).

p. 348. *Writing.* The notion of 'write and hide away' is found in the *Confessions* of Jean-Jacques Rousseau (1712–78). Rousseau believed that one needed to withdraw from society in order to write; that truth could be found and formulated only in solitude.

p. 350. *Reflection. Les Chimères* (1854) is the famous collection of sonnets by Gérard de Nerval.

p. 355. *French Clarity.* 'What is conceived well is expressed clearly', a well-known maxim formulated by Nicolas Boileau (1636–1711) in *L'Art poétique* (1674).

p. 355. *Unexplainable.* 'Because he was he and I was I' is a famous quotation taken from Montaigne's essay 'On Friendship' (1580).

p. 355. *I.* The German artist Caspar David Friedrich (1774–1840) painted *Der Mönch am Meer* (*The Monk by the Sea*) between 1808 and 1810.

p. 357. *Rough Drafts.* I have employed 'Sleepy Hollow' (Washington Irving's story *The Legend of Sleepy Hollow*, 1820) to translate Chappuis's punning allusion to 'Bois dormant'. The latter makes the French readers think of *La Belle au bois dormant* ('Sleeping Beauty')—a tale published by Charles Perrault in 1697. Chappuis casts his focus on the 'sleeping woods', not on the 'sleeping beauty'.

p. 358. *Speaking.* 'It speaks for itself' is a translation of the French expression 'c'est parlant'. Paul Éluard's line 'One dreams about a poem as one dreams about a human being' comes from 'L'évidence poétique', a lecture given in London on 24 June 1936, at the International Surrealist Exhibition.

p. 359. *Space and Movement.* Claude Lorrain (1600–82), whose real name was Claude Gellée, was a French painter of the Baroque era. His masterpieces have influenced landscape painters of the eighteenth and nineteenth centuries.

ACKNOWLEDGEMENTS

The translator would like to express his gratitude to the editors of the following magazines and anthologies for first publishing several of these translated poems:

Modern and Contemporary Swiss Poetry: An Anthology (Luzius Keller ed.). London: Dalkey Archive Press, 2012.

The Bitter Oleander (Fall 2013 and Spring 2014). Available at: www.bitteroleander.com

International Literary Quarterly (Autumn 2013). Available at: www.interlitq.org

Two Lines (online) as well as the print edition (September 2014). Available at: www.catranslation.org/two-lines-online

The Plume Anthology of Poetry 2013 (Daniel Lawless ed.). Asheville, NC: MadHat Press, 2014.

Colony (Spring 2014). Available at: www.colonyeditors.-wix.com/colony#!translation/c22g5

Catamaran Literary Reader (Spring 2014). Available at: www.catamaranliteraryreader.com/index-3

The Fortnightly Review (September 2014). Available at: www.fortnightlyreview.co.uk

Skidrow Penthouse 17 (2014). Available at: www.skidrowpenthouse.com/pdfs/SRP.SRP17.layout.pdf